A volume in the Hyperion reprint series

THE RADICAL TRADITION IN AMERICA

HYPERION PRESS, INC.

Westport, Connecticut

TOOLS AND THE MAN

PROPERTY AND INDUSTRY UNDER THE CHRISTIAN LAW

BY

WASHINGTON GLADDEN

May it please your Serene Highnesses, your Majesties, Lordships, and Law-wardships, the proper Epic of this world is not now "Arms and the Man;" how much less "Shirt-frills and the Man;" no, it is now "Tools and the Man;" that, henceforth to all time, is now our Epic; — and you, first of all others, I think, were wise to take note of that. — CARLYLE, Past and Present.

BOSTON AND NEW YORK
HOUGHTON, MIFFLIN AND COMPANY
The Riverside Press, Cambridge
1893

Published in 1893 by Houghton, Mifflin and Company, Boston

Hyperion reprint edition 1975
Library of Congress Catalog Number 75-353
ISBN 0-88355-222-1
Printed in the United States of America
Note: To enhance readability, the type of this edition has been enlarged 20% from the smaller size of the original.

Library of Congress Cataloging in Publication Data

Gladden, Washington, 1836-1918.
Tools and the man.

(The Radical tradition in America)
Reprint of the 1893 ed. published by Houghton, Mifflin, Boston, in series: Lyman Beecher lectures, 1886-87.
1. Economics. 2. Sociology, Christian. 3. Socialism, Christian. I. Title. II. Series: Lyman Beecher lectures; 1886-87.
HB171.G49 1975 261.8'5 75-353
ISBN 0-88355-222-1

PREFACE.

THE chapters which follow contain the substance of a course of lectures spoken to the students of the New Haven Theological Seminary, on the Lyman Beecher foundation, in January, 1887. Portions of the same course have been given in Cornell University, in Mansfield College, Oxford University, and in other places. In November and December, 1892, they were reconstructed and delivered before the Meadville Theological School and the citizens of Meadville, Pa. Of this last use of them some explanation should be made: —

The Rev. Adin Ballou, of Hopedale, Mass., left a legacy for the promotion of Christian Socialism, to the interests of which he had devoted a life of energetic philanthropy. Through some legal defects in the bequest, the courts refused to execute his will, and the property passed into the hands of his daughter, Mrs. Abbie Ballou Heywood. Determined to carry out her father's purposes, Mrs.

Heywood made over the entire amount to the trustees of the Meadville Theological School, to be held by them as a trust fund for the establishment and maintenance of "THE ADIN BALLOU LECTURESHIP OF PRACTICAL CHRISTIAN SOCIOLOGY." The design of the founder is thus expressed in her own words: —

"The purpose of this offer is to secure the annual delivery of a course of lectures, by the most satisfactory talent that can be obtained, upon *the social aspects of the religion of Christ, and the consequent duty and importance of applying the principles and spirit of that religion to the intercourse and conduct of man with man, in all the activities and relations of life.* In these lectures special attention shall be paid to such subjects, for example, as 'The Barbarism of War and the consequent claims of the cause of Peace,' 'The Extinction of the Evils of Intemperance,' 'The Proper Relation of the Sexes, including the true Doctrine of Marriage and Divorce,' 'The Higher Education and Complete Enfranchisement of Woman,' 'The Adjustment and Harmonization of the Relations between Capital and Labor,' 'The Prevention of and Remedy for Poverty,' 'The Care and Reformation of Criminals,' 'The Amelioration and Improvement of the Condition of the Unfortunate and Perishing Classes,' including in their full range all topics calculated to enhance the well-being and happiness of mankind and to fashion human society after the Christian ideal of the kingdom of heaven on earth.

"These lectures, or such of them as may be deemed most valuable by the President and Board of Instruction, shall be published from time to time, and sent, free of expense, to other Theological Schools, and to leading educational institutions, libraries, etc., to the end that their usefulness may be extended as far and wide as possible.

"It is furthermore my express wish and intention that the contemplated lectureship shall be based upon *the distinct and positive recognition of the eternal excellency of the religion of Christ, in its fundamental truth and essential spirit,* as taught and exemplified in the Scriptures of the New Testament, and as interpreted by the light of the advancing intelligence of mankind, and that its administration shall be absolutely impartial and free, regardless alike of denominational peculiarities and limitations, and of all artificial distinctions of race, sex, and nationality.

"This offer is made with the full expectation and assurance that, if accepted, the endowment involved will be held sacred to the purpose for which it is designed, and in the earnest hope that the work of human improvement and social regeneration, so dear to the heart of my beloved father, will be advanced by the instrumentality it provides for and ordains, and that his name and influence for good in the world may be conserved and perpetuated unto many generations."

This volume comprises the first course of lectures upon the Adin Ballou foundation. A portion of one of them has appeared in print; the remainder is now for the first time published.

My own deepest convictions are so clearly expressed in the words quoted above that I have found no difficulty in following the lines laid down by the founder. By the study and observation of many years, I have been confirmed in the belief that the Christian law, when rightly interpreted, contains the solution of the social problem. I believe that Christianity not only holds up before us a beautiful ideal, but that it presents the only theory of industrial and social order which can be made to work. To the arguments which follow, in support of this opinion, I ask the serious attention of all men of good-will.

W. G.

First Congregational Church,
Columbus, Ohio, *Feb.* 22, 1893.

CONTENTS.

TOOLS AND THE MAN.

I.

THE CHRISTIANIZATION OF SOCIETY.

THE end of Christianity is twofold, a perfect man in a perfect society. These purposes are never separated; they cannot be separated. No man can be redeemed and saved alone; no community can be reformed and elevated save as the individuals of which it is composed are regenerated. The law and the gospel address themselves to the conscience and the affection of the man, but they address him as a member of the social organism, and the response that he makes must be made through the medium of that organism. What says the law to him? Thou shalt love the Lord thy God with all thy heart, and thou shalt love thy neighbor as thyself. Perfection requires perfect obedience to the second commandment as well as to the first. If there were a man who had no neighbor, he could not obey God's law; he could not be a man, in any proper sense of the word; he could not exercise the powers and functions of the human nature; the perfection of manhood would be utterly beyond his attainment. This vital and necessary relation of the individual to society lies at the basis of the Christian conception of life. Christianity would create a perfect society, and to this end it must produce perfect men; it would bring forth perfect men, and to this end it must construct a perfect society.

Christ's first word as a preacher was, Repent. That was addressed to the individual. It was the reproof of his sin; it was the summons to that choice of righteousness which is the prerogative of a free personality. But his next word was connected with this by a copula that we must never break: "Repent; *for* the kingdom of heaven is at hand." The opportunity, the motive, the condition of repentance is the presence of a divine society, of which the penitent, by virtue of his penitence, at once becomes a member.

The first commandment of the new dispensation is, therefore, a commandment with promise, and the commandment can never be divorced from the promise. Life implies an environment, the continuous adjustment of external and internal relations. Everything that lives, lives in some element to which its nature is adapted. The fish lives in the water; the man lives in an atmosphere. The spiritual life is no exception to this law. When a man is born of the spirit, he needs a spiritual atmosphere to breathe as truly as he needs the vital air the moment he is born into the world. True it is that except a man be born from above he cannot see the kingdom of

God; but equally true it is that if there were not a kingdom of God for him to be born into, his birthday would be the day of his death. To bid a man repent without furnishing him at the same time a spiritual society in which he may live and move and have his being would be like ordering a man who was stifling in bad air to betake himself to a vacuum. Such unreasoning cruelty our Lord does not countenance; when he calls men to new life he surrounds them with the conditions in which the new life is possible.

When Jesus commissions the twelve and sends them forth, he puts into their mouths the same message that he himself first proclaimed, save that he omits the first word "Repent." "As ye go, preach, saying, The kingdom of heaven is at hand." I am not inclined to attach any peculiar significance to this omission. Doubtless the word of repentance and reformation was part of their message, though not here specified. They were bidden to preach the truth which he had taught them; what they had heard in the ear they were to proclaim upon the housetops, and the call to repentance was surely included in this. Nevertheless, the fact remains that in this commission the emphasis is put upon the proclamation of the kingdom of God. "As ye go, preach, saying, The kingdom of heaven is at hand." It is not a remote and dubious inference that the regeneration of the individual and the regeneration of society are coördinate interests; that the one cannot be secured without the other; that, whatever the order of logic may be, there can be no difference in time between the two kinds of work; that we are to labor as constantly and as diligently for the improvement of the social order as for the conversion of man.

The success of our Christian work largely depends, indeed, upon maintaining the equilibrium between these two kinds of activity. Progress is often conditioned upon preserving the balance of equal forces; many of the losses and delays of civilization are due to the failure to secure this equipoise. The Greek republics sacrificed the individual to the state, and perished for that fault; the modern radical democracy has sacrificed the state to the individual, and threatens us with destruction from this cause. In practical statesmanship, it is not easy to adjust the opposing claims of liberty and order. The Roman Catholic church minimizes the individual and magnifies the ecclesiastical organization; many of our Protestant churches foster an excessive development of individualism and greatly undervalue social forces and institutional methods.

There is need among us, then, of emphasizing the social side of our Christian work, of pointing out the fact that Christianity gives a law to society as well as to the individual. We are called to convert men, and we are called at the same time and with equal authority to furnish them a Christian society to live in after they are converted. It is idle and even cruel for us to cry, "Repent," unless we can truly say at the same time, "The kingdom of heaven is at hand."

In a recent admirable essay upon "Social Ethics" I find this passage: "[Christianity] teaches that men owe it to each other to labor, not first for the improvement of outward conditions, but first for the worth and goodness of men themselves, according to the high and definite standards of the Christian character. Christianity is not satisfied with mere improvement upon the existing order, nor will it turn aside and expend its energies on reforms which affect only the surface of society." In terms this is exactly true; nevertheless, it needs to be supplemented by a fuller statement. There are certain outward conditions, certain forms of social organization, which tend to emphasize and promote the worth and goodness of men themselves; and there are other outward conditions which tend to belittle and discourage personal worth and goodness. There is a social philosophy, an economical philosophy, which disparages and ignores character; it gets itself incorporated into outward conditions; it makes the problem of arousing and developing men themselves a very difficult business. Now, while the ends of character are above all things precious, *because* they are above all things precious, we need to encourage those forms of social organization in which the value of character shall be rightly estimated, and men shall not be reckoned merely as counters in the great game of material exchanges.

The christianization of society is, therefore, a part, and a large part, of the calling of the disciples and servants of Jesus Christ. The kingdoms of this world are to become the kingdoms of our Lord and of his Christ; and the phrase includes not merely the kingdom of Siam, and the kingdom of Madagascar, and tho kingdom of Dahomey, but the kingdom of commerce, and the kingdom of industry, and the kingdom of fashion, and the kingdom of learning, and the kingdom of amusement; every great department of society is to be pervaded by the Christian spirit and governed by Christian law. This is the end that we are to set before ourselves, and toward the achievement of which we are to direct our energies.

1. The christianization of society involves the christianization of the prevailing social sentiments. "Social sentiment," says Dr. Bascom, "is the pervasive protoplasm of general and individual life. From this must come the constructive and beneficent forces of the state, and largely the impulses which govern each individual within the state."[1]

The best society differs from the worst in its practices, its institutions, its laws, but more deeply and radically in its sentiments. It is because song is the voice of sentiment that the philosopher said, "Let me make the songs of a people, and I care not who makes its laws." Now, there are social sentiments that are distinctively Christian, and

[1] *The Words of Christ*, p. 198.

others that are as clearly unchristian, and it is part of our work to propagate those that are Christian, and extirpate those that are not. Respect for character more than for rank or wealth is a Christian sentiment. "A man's life consisteth not in the abundance of the things which he possesseth," said the Teacher. Honor for honest industry is a Christian sentiment; no follower of the Judean Carpenter can be in doubt about that. Compassion for the suffering and the helpless is a Christian sentiment. *Noblesse oblige* is a Christian sentiment; who was it that washed his disciples' feet? The prevalence in society of sentiments like these makes it peaceful, pure, and stimulating; every soul that breathes this atmosphere is comforted and quickened and ennobled by it. On the other hand, the sentiments opposed to these, when they prevail in society, as they often do, fill it with envy and strife and bitterness; every generous feeling is chilled by such a social atmosphere. Now, it is quite possible for us, in our social intercourse, to aid in cultivating these Christian sentiments, and in exterminating those which are unchristian. We are called, as disciples of Christ, to the frank and hearty utterance of Christian sentiments, and to the equally positive repudiation of those that are unchristian. If you respect the upright brakeman more than the gambling and swindling general manager, say it and show it. If you feel that the true-hearted shop-girl who supports herself and her mother by her labor is more to be admired than the giggling flirt who is doing nothing but waste her father's substance in frivolous follies, make that feeling clearly manifest. Opportunities are hourly occurring for the utterance of the thoughts and feelings by which our estimate of life and conduct is revealed, and a manly avowal of the truth that is in us, that has become part of ourselves, often has a most salutary influence. We are not merely to think on the things that are honest and pure and lovely and of good report; we are to stand up for them, to declare our love for them, to defend them by word and act when others cast contempt upon them. There is a great deal of good missionary work to be done in reforming the sentiments of the society in which we live, — to be done in drawing-rooms and church-aisles, in school-rooms and shops and street-cars, wherever men and women meet and greet one another; and here, as much as anywhere, our Master wants brave confessors and true witnesses.

2. Sentiments that have crystallized into maxims or formularies take the shape of theories. The relations of individuals and of classes in society are defined by social theories; there are theories of social duty and obligation, some of which conform to the Christian law, and many of which do not. One very large part of our duty as citizens of the kingdom of heaven is to test these social theories by the law of that kingdom; to uphold those that agree with it, and to renounce and con-

demn those that do not. Bad practice has its roots in bad philosophy; and the social disorder and mischief that abound will never be corrected until the false social philosophy which breeds them is exposed. A social theory was in vogue not very long ago, in all parts of Christendom, that some human beings are born to be the chattels of other human beings; that this division of the race into masters and slaves is one of the laws of nature, and part of the plan of Providence. That theory was contrary to the great doctrine of human brotherhood, which is the corner-stone of Christian society. It was necessary to kill that theory before society could be christianized.

There is a theory which finds wide acceptance in these days, to the effect that when husband and wife conclude that they cannot get along very well together they ought to be divorced. This theory has been making great havoc in society of late, breaking up homes and weakening the bonds of the family, which is the very foundation of society. It expressly contradicts the Christian law; and one of the most urgent duties resting upon Christian disciples at the present time is to expose the sophistry and wickedness of this doctrine of easy divorce, and lift up against it Christ's law of the family.

Not a few pernicious social theories must be corrected and counteracted by the application of the Christian law; and, on the other hand, there are many wise and salutary social maxims that ought to be diligently inculcated, the truth and wisdom of which will gradually be made manifest if they are faithfully taught. The theory that all property is held in trust for society; that there is no such thing as absolute ownership; that every possessor of wealth, no matter how lawfully he may have gained it, holds it as a steward or a trustee, and is bound to use it for the best interest of the society in which he lives, — this is a part of the clear teaching of Christ which must be steadily enforced. Society will never be christianized until this truth is accepted and reduced to practice.

These examples, which might be multiplied, and will be in the chapters that follow, show that there is a Christian philosophy of social relations which differs widely in many respects from the prevailing social philosophy; and that our business as servants of Christ is to challenge the sensual and selfish philosophy so widely prevalent, and to supplant it by the doctrine of the kingdom of heaven.

3. When social theories are reduced to practice, we call them customs. A large part of social life is customary. Our sentiments and theories are organized into these living forms, and are thus unconsciously communicated from one life to another, and transmitted from generation to generation. Many of these social customs are already Christian, and among the mightiest conquests that Christianity has achieved is the silent and gradual transformation of the usages and conventions of society by the inward working of its power. How

much there is in our customary life that expresses good will! How many of our forms of etiquette are only transcriptions of the law of love! And not only benevolence, but justice and purity and modesty and many other Christian virtues find expression in social conventions to which we have been habituated all our lives. Probably none of us is aware of the extent to which his life has been influenced by these organized forms of life which surround him like an atmosphere. Yet there are many existing social customs which are not Christian, — which are the reverse of Christian. There are still vast spaces of this customary life which need to be subdued and informed by the spirit of Christ. Customs that are pernicious, destructive, heathenish, abound in most communities, and there is need that the law of Christ should be applied to them, and that they should be made to feel the steady weight of its condemnation. Yet, in judging all these, we must be careful to discern the real meaning of the law, and beware how we substitute for it our own whims and prejudices. There are various evil customs, like the drinking usages, and the gambling practices, and the unhealthy excesses of all sorts, which still prevail in some quarters, and against which the Christian moralist must utter a clear testimony; and there are other social customs, innocent enough in themselves, but liable to abuse, and of these he must learn to speak with discrimination. Perhaps there is no part of his work in which a judicial temper is more necessary than in the criticism of social customs. He must make the truth he speaks manifest to the consciences of those to whom he speaks; he must beware lest he make that to be sin which is not sin, and load the moral sense of those who hear him with a burden that they will not bear. Great wisdom is needed here, but the law of Christ applies to this realm of life as well as to every other, and it must be possible to bring its truth to bear upon the customs of society so as to condemn those that are evil, and approve those that are good.

4. Customs that are organized under definite and permanent forms are institutions. The institutions of civilized society are its vital organs; it lives in them and by them. The family is the first of these; the church, the schools, the various organizations for industrial purposes, for culture, for pleasure, for charity, are numbered among them. For every one of these institutions the great Lawgiver has a law; it is for his disciples to discern and reveal the manner of its application. Most of these established forms of social life recognize to some extent the ethics of Christ, and embody more or less perfectly the precepts and principles of his teaching in their organic life. Yet there is not one of them that completely and consistently conforms to his law; not one of them that does not need to be christianized. The church is supposed to be organized upon Christ's words, and to be the embodiment of his life. Of

the ideal church, of the invisible church, this is true ; of the visible church it is only partially true. A great deal of the teaching, the administration, the corporate life of the church is unchristian; the kingdom of God, which Jesus came to establish in the world, is divided against itself and crippled in its growth in many places through organizations calling themselves churches. True it is that the church, in most communities, contains the greater part of the moral force existing in those communities ; the only hope for the reformation of society is in the church ; if society is christianized, it must be done mainly through the church ; yet it is no less true that the church is everywhere part of the thing to be reformed, and that the institution which represents Christ in the world and speaks for him is an institution that discerns his mind but in part, and that reflects his spirit as in a mirror darkly. Every church needs prayerfully to ask itself how much of its doctrine, its discipline, its practice, needs christianizing. Part of its business is to criticise the social order; but it should never forget, in its criticisms of the social order, that judgment should begin at the house of God. Surely the church that deliberately proposes to be a church of the wealthy and cultivated classes; that makes no provision for the poor in its assemblies ; that tolerates arrangements in its place of worship under which the poor could not find a home in it if they would ; that openly says, "These poor people can come to our church, of course, if they wish to come, but frankly we think that they would enjoy themselves more in a mission chapel down on one of the back streets, and we shall be happy to contribute toward the building of such a chapel for them," — a church like this really needs to do a good deal of home mission work within its own four walls before it will be prepared to assist very materially in the christianization of society.

There are many other features of the social life of some of our churches which very imperfectly conform to the Christian ideal, and those who are responsible for the conduct of the churches ought to consider more carefully than they sometimes do what manner of organization a Christian church ought to be; what should be the relation of its members one to another, what the ordering of its assemblies, what the spirit of its appeal to the world outside. There is a sense in which a church may think too much about itself: it may expend all its energies in building up its own organization; it may care for those that are without only in so far as there is a fair prospect of bringing them within, and so adding to its own popularity and power. Human nature often takes on this phase, in churches as well as in secret lodges and political parties. But there is another way in which a church does well to think much about itself: it ought continually to compare its own internal life with the Sermon on the Mount; it ought to seek to develop its life in accordance with that high, unworldly standard. Every true pastor should be admonished to keep this matter very near his own heart. The spirit of the world outside is always insensibly pervading the church; its pride, its indifference, its exclusiveness, its methods of competition, first steal in and hide, and then stalk in and take possession; and there is need of coming back to first principles very often, and of reminding ourselves whose disciples we are, and what is the nature of the kingdom that he came to found. And the earnest pastor will find it in his heart to say very often, Dearly beloved brethren, let us remember that we are Christians; let us try to behave in the house of God as though we were Christians; let us show all men, rich or poor, who come into our place of worship that we are Christians; let us meet one another on the street as though we were Christians; let us put ourselves into such relations with all other churches that they shall know that we are Christians; let us speak to our neighbors round about us a message of such invincible friendliness that they shall be constrained to believe that we are Christians, that we have been with Jesus. If the life that is in us is thus manifestly the life of Christ, and the bond that unites us is the love of Christ, we shall surely be able to do some good work in christianizing society. We can never accomplish much as a church in this direction unless we can make it evident that Christ is not only the Head, but also the Heart of the body that claims to represent him.

If the church needs thus to apply to itself the perfect standard of Christ's law in order that its faults may be corrected and its social life properly developed, it is not probable that any other of the institutions of society could wisely dispense with such criticism. To bring all these institutions into conformity with the Christian law, and to fill them all with the Christian spirit, is the work before us, — a work so vast that we might well turn away from it in despair, had we not the assurance that when, in the regeneration, the Son of Man shall come in his glory, these kingdoms, too, shall belong to him.

5. Above all the social institutions the state is supreme. It is as truly divine as the church is, and its scope is more comprehensive. It is the business of the state to declare and maintain upon the earth the righteousness of God; could there be a more august vocation? Christ as Prophet and Priest is the Head of the church, as King he is the Head of the state. His kingly office is his supreme office. Messiah, the King, he always claimed to be. True it is that the King has not yet come to his own; but a great voice has been heard saying, "I will overturn, overturn, overturn it . . . until he come whose right it is, and I will give it him." The state is to be christianized. Government is to be christianized, not by the restoration of the temporal power, not by calling back the Pope or the Puritans, but by the exaltation and coronation of the spiritual power, the true spiritual power, in

the hearts and lives of the people. Most true is the word of Immanuel H. Fichte, "Christianity is destined some day to be the inner organizing power of the state."[1]

Our laws are to be christianized; the time is coming when they will express the perfect justice and the perfect beneficence of the Christian law.

Our notion of what government ought to be is to be christianized. For when "All-of-us," or even The-great-majority-of-us, get into our heads Christ's notion of what it means to rule, we shall find some better thing to do than simply to keep The-rest-of-us from breaking into our houses and robbing our hen-roosts. When the King of us all does come to his own, you will discover that he is something more than a policeman.

The administration of government is to be christianized. We are to have in our magistracies, in our places of power and trust and judgment, upright men, honorable men, — when the word of the Son of Jesse shall be verified in all the earth:

> "One that ruleth over men righteously,
> That ruleth in the fear of God,
> He shall be as the light of the morning, when the sun riseth,
> A morning without clouds."

Doubtless this millennial perfection of state is yet a great way off, but it is the goal toward which we are journeying, and we are to keep it always before our thought, and to stretch forward unto it with dauntless faith and unfailing purpose. This work

[1] Quoted by Bascom, *The Words of Christ*, p. 191.

of christianizing our governments, national, state, municipal, seems, indeed, a herculean labor; but it is one of the most immediate and most urgent of all our Christian duties. Into that realm of sophistry and perversity and brutality which men call politics we are to pour a steady stream of honest testimony and unselfish effort; the viler is that pool, the greater is the need that a strong and steady current of intelligence and conscience flow through it for its cleansing. The kingdom of God can never come in its power while governments are corrupt, and the spirit of party makes men reckless of the interests of truth and justice. One of the clear signs of its coming, when it comes, will be better government; and those who pray for its coming must use the power that they have in bringing it nearer. Inasmuch as government is the most comprehensive and the most powerful of all the institutions of society; inasmuch as it presses upon the moral life of men in a thousand ways continually, shaping their ideals, directing their choices, calling forth or repressing their activities, it is evident that the christianizing of society will be greatly promoted or greatly hindered by the existing government. No one who desires to behold the progress of Christian morality can be indifferent to the character of the government under which he lives.

So much as this must then be involved in this promised christianization of society, — that the sentiments, theories, customs, institutions, laws, and governments of the people are to be penetrated with the Christian spirit, founded on Christian principles, ruled by the Christian law. This is what is meant by the coming to earth of the kingdom of heaven. We pray every day that it may come, but we do not by this prayer imply that its advent is still to be awaited. He who taught us to utter this prayer had already proclaimed, "The kingdom of heaven is at hand!" It was present then, this divine society, this kingdom of truth and love; and the centuries have but enlarged its dominion and confirmed its peaceful sway. Mighty have been the changes wrought through its gentle influence; the world in which we live is a vastly better world than the brightest dream of the best man who had lived in the world two thousand years ago. Through faithful witnesses, through brave confessors, through loyal soldiers of the cross, Christian truth and love have been steadily gaining possession of the hearts of men and of the life of society; the opinions, the feelings, the maxims, the usages, the organized activities of men have been gradually suffused with Christian motives and principles; the leaven has been working silently but pervasively upon the mass. When we behold what has been done already, we return with faith and courage to the work which remains to do.

Only let us keep it steadily before us that this is our work. There is a conception of Christian service which differs from this very widely. In this conception, the office of Christ and the work of his church is merely to gather the few that can be saved out of the wreck of humanity, and let the rest go to destruction. There is no hope of the transformation of society through the use of any agencies or forces now known to us; society must go more and more swiftly to decay; social sentiments, philosophies, practices, institutions, will grow more corrupt and godless continually; it is useless for us to try to improve them; all that is left for us is to get as many as we can out of this evil society, keep them apart from it as much as we can while they live, and see them safe through this world to heaven.

Now, this is a theory with which it is necessary for us to come at once to a definite understanding. If this theory is true, all that we have been saying is visionary and chimerical. No man who believes this theory works for the christianization of society; he does not hope for it. He may labor for the conversion of souls, but he has no faith in the regeneration of social sentiments, practices, institutions. It is the destruction, not the sanctification, of the social order that he is looking for. He may bid men repent; but if he tells them that the kingdom of heaven is at hand, he does not mean by these words what we have been assuming them to mean, that it is actually here, growing as the mustard-tree grows, from frailest germ to goodliest stature, — silently pervading and transforming the human world as the leaven pervades and transforms the mass; he means, rather, that there is presently to be expected a great revolution by which the existing order shall be demolished and swept out of existence. He may have a kind of missionary zeal, but his work will be purely individual, and not in any broad sense institutional; for no existing social institution except the church does he entertain any hope, and not even for that.

It is evident at once that the vocation of a Christian church, as conceived by one who holds this theory, or any theory akin to this, will differ widely from the one assumed in this discussion. It is evident that the activities of two churches, one of which holds one of these theories, and the other the opposite, will follow widely different lines. The fundamental commands of Christ will be interpreted by one in a sense radically unlike that of the other.

Take, for example, the commandment, "Seek ye first the kingdom of God, and his righteousness." What does this signify? Where is the kingdom of God? If we are to seek it, some hint must be given us of the quarter in which we are to look. Is it present, accessible, visible to men? So Christ seems to teach. It is "at hand," he says. We are not to be rummaging the centuries and scouring the continents in search of it; it is near us. We are not to be crying, Lo, here! or Lo, there! for the kingdom of God is among us. Yet he implies that some spiritual perception is needed to discern it. Except a man be born from above he cannot *see* the kingdom of God. Not merely will he fail to enter into it; he will not even perceive it. One must be naturalized in that divine society, or he may not be aware of its existence; he may be living in the midst of it, and not know it. There are others besides the young man at Dothan who need to have their eyes opened that they may perceive the presence of spiritual hosts round about them.

This is why we are bidden to seek the kingdom of God, — not because it is remote, or hidden, but because our vision needs training; the power of discerning it is what we want most. It is here; the one thing needful is that we should realize its presence and fall into line with its mighty ongoings.

A vital question is this, whether the Parousia of Christ is his presence or his future arrival from some distant scene; our characters and our services will be greatly affected by the answer we give it. If we believe that he is here, now, building his kingdom, our thoughts, our hopes, our labors, will take on forms quite different from those which they would assume if we believed that he was not here, but that his coming was to be awaited, in some indefinite future. If he is here building his kingdom, we shall surely find traces of his working, signs of his power, — such as we have just been considering. When we find these, we shall thank God and take courage; we shall see that our daily prayer is being answered; we shall work with new hope for the fuller bringing in of the glory of the kingdom. If, on the other hand, we assume that he is not here, we shall not be looking for any tokens of his presence; the changes that are taking place will not reveal him to our thought; we shall see no beauty in them; we shall ascribe them to other agencies; we shall regard them with indifference, perhaps with critical contempt. Here lies the peril. It is a fearful thing to repudiate and decry what God hath wrought with infinite love and wisdom through the long centuries of his patience. It is a dismal and dreadful spectacle to see men standing in the dawn of this new day and crying that there is no light. Strangely do they honor their Master and Lord when they fail to discern anything but evil in the bright displays of his power of which the world is full.

Let us learn that the calling of the Christian disciple is no such dispiriting vocation. We are not the forlorn hope of a lost cause, struggling with desperate valor to rescue a few helpless prisoners out of the hands of a victorious foe. We are not the followers of a Leader who has signally failed in his mission, and who now finds no resource but to destroy a world that he is not strong enough to save. We believe that the kingdom, and the dominion, and the greatness of the kingdom under the whole heaven belong to the servants of our King; that his kingdom is an everlasting kingdom; that all dominions shall serve and obey him, and that he is steadily and surely advancing to the possession of the inheritance that belongs to him; and we deem it our duty to claim it for him, and to do what we can, while we are here, to bring the day when at the name of Jesus every knee shall bow, of things in heaven and things in earth, and things under the earth, and every tongue shall confess that He is Lord, to the glory of God the Father

II.

ECONOMICS AND CHRISTIAN ETHICS.

THE warrior bold whose heart has been stirred with the enthusiasm of humanity, and who goes forth to do battle for the christianization of society, finds his first and perhaps his most formidable foe in the great realm of industry and trade. All that great department of life is yet in large measure unsubdued by the power of the Christ. His august voice has been heard in its noisy marts, and his whip of small cords has driven forth some of the worst of the money-changers; the influence of Christian ethics upon the industrial and commercial realm has been perceptible and beneficent; but that realm still remains in great part intractable, if not hostile, to his gentle sway. The desire of property, which, if it is not the earliest of the constitutional desires to find development, soon becomes stronger and more universal than any of the rest, is the one overmastering passion of modern society. Our individualistic régime has given it free play; it has been the great builder of civilization on its material side; it has cleared the forests, drained the swamps, dug the mines, bridged the rivers, set the spindles and the pistons and the lathes and the trip-hammers in motion, built the great cities, covered the continents with networks of steel, and turned the ocean into a ferry. Great are the gains of this master passion; swift and splendid are the triumphs it has won; but the very suddenness of these achievements should seem to us ominous. Enduring good is not wont thus to spring up, gourd-like, in a night. It begins to be evident to thoughtful minds that the social structure which our unbridled egoism has been building is not in all respects well built; that its foundations are insecure, and that its walls are full of inflammable and explosive material; that unless something is done, and that speedily, to protect and preserve it, the catastrophe may be sudden and terrible. A single egoistic passion like this, when it takes possession of a people or an age, can create wonders, and it can destroy them quite as speedily. The problem now before us is, whether any higher power can be invoked to save the good that the greed of gain has brought forth upon the earth. This is the problem that confronts those who labor for the christianization of society.

The enormous inequalities of condition and possessions existing and constantly increasing among us foster, on both sides of the great gulf, — among the rich as well as among the poor, — tempers and sentiments which are the reverse of Christian. Contempt on the one side, envy on the other, fill the social atmosphere with feverish and inflammable influences. Inequalities perhaps as great have existed in other ages; but never before such inequalities in a society founded on the doctrine that all men are created equal in rights and privileges; never before in a society in which the poor had the spelling-book and the newspaper and the ballot in their hands; never before in a society where the penniless walked every day before show windows wherein all the luxuries of all the climes were publicly displayed. Between the helots of Greece and their masters, between the slaves and the citizens of Rome, there was really no contrast, because there was no comparison; they were supposed to belong to distinct orders of creation. Aristotle classes the slaves of a household as belonging with the tools, the instruments of production. There are tools with souls, and tools without souls; yet the soul of this tool is not, he says, like the soul of its owner; it is a soul without a will. Ulpian, the Stoic, speaks of "slaves and other animals." Even the lofty mind of Marcus Aurelius has no higher thought about them; they are enumerated along with the cattle. Such was the universal sentiment, and the slaves themselves could scarcely have disputed the theory of society that had sent them under the yoke. If they had nothing but chains and servitude, and their lords and masters had nothing but idleness and luxury, that was the order of nature, the condition to which they were born, and from which it was idle, if not impious, to try to escape. Inequalities in that ancient society could not, therefore, have been such a constant source of irritation as they are in modern society. Servile insurrections did, indeed, now and then occur, showing that these tools with souls were sometimes skeptical about the philosophy that consigned them to bondage, and were prone to think, in spite of Aristotle, that they had wills of their own; but the voice of the great world denounced their pretensions and drowned their protests, and they soon laid down their weapons and returned to the servile condition from which they had vainly striven to rise.

It is a very different undertaking to convince the poor laborers of America and England that the social chasm which divides them from their luxurious neighbors is one that has been fixed by nature. They have been taught equality of rights; they cannot easily accept so great inequality of conditions and possessions. And the spectacle of wealth and want steadily increasing side by side, wealth growing more insolent and want more hopeless, year by year, fills them with discontent and bitterness. I will not now discuss the question how far these poor laborers are themselves responsible for their poverty. I only note the fact that the poverty of great multitudes exists in the midst of rapidly growing wealth; and that a consequence of this inequality is social alienation and enmity, which renders the christianization of society a very difficult task.

Not only does this strife exist between the rich and the poor, between the employing and the employed; the commercial world is also the arena of sharp and bitter conflicts. Rivals in trade are seeking to overreach or undermine one another; competitors are struggling for exclusive privileges; merchants are trying to force one another out of the market; great companies or corporations are sometimes striving to crush one another, and sometimes combining to crush the smaller corporations. On all sides, a fierce greed and a conscienceless purpose keep society in a restless, jealous, antipathetic temper.

Surely this great realm of industry and traffic, with its glaring inequalities of condition, its extremes of wealth and poverty, its bitter resentments and envyings, its greedy rivalries and competitions, is yet far from being christianized. The law of this realm is not yet, "Thou shalt love thy neighbor as thyself." The commandment which bids us look not after our own interests exclusively, but after the interests of others also, is not a ruling maxim in this kingdom of exchanges.

Is it possible to christianize this realm of toil and traffic? Is it reasonable to hope that the time will ever come when the great majority of those who buy and sell, who hire work and work for hire, will put away the weapons of their warfare, and endeavor to do to others as they would have others do to them? Doubtless the prospect of such a day is distant enough to be enchanting; but it were a sorry confession that no such thing could be hoped for. That would signify that Christianity is a failure. No more damaging accusation could be made than this. If our King stands powerless before the power of Mammon, we cannot crown him Lord of all. Some of us are not yet ready to make this confession. We still profess to believe that the kingdoms of this world belong to him, and are yet to be brought under his dominion. And they to whom the meaning of Christ's mission has been clearly made manifest are girding themselves now as never before for the conflict on this great battlefield.

When we enlist for this campaign, voices are heard protesting. This domain of industry and traffic, they tell us, is not within the province of Christianity. It is possible that Christianity might do something to soften the asperities and sweeten the tempers of contending parties in this arena; but the law that rules in all this realm is not the law of Christ; it is the law of self-interest; if any attempt should be made to apply Christian ethics to the relation between master and workman, between seller and buyer, confusion would arise at once; the Christian law may be the best law for the home and the school and the neighborhood, but it will never work in the factory or the market; benevolence and generosity and unselfishness are good enough in their place, but business is business. You know that this is the common sentiment of the street and the exchange, but it is more than this: it is the doctrine of what has been widely known as science; it is the fundamental assumption of a reasoned philosophy of economics which has been current over a large part of the world for almost a century. No clearer contradiction can be expressed in logical terms than that by which certain teachers of political economy have denied the validity of Christ's law, and have asserted the exact contrary of that which his law affirms. It lies at the basis of the great work of Adam Smith upon the "Wealth of Nations" that self-interest is the one supremely beneficent social force; that when every man seeks his own with all his might the whole world will be prosperous and happy. The supremacy of self-interest over benevolence is everywhere assumed, and the absolute sufficiency of this principle, if unobstructed, to promote human welfare is regarded as too plain for argument. The *a priori* assumption, "half theological, half metaphysical," on which his whole argument rests is, as Professor Ingram has stated, the notion that when the individual aims only at his private gain, he is led by an invisible hand to promote the public good.[1] Obviously, then, it is the duty of the individual to aim only at his private gain; the most unswerving egoism is the truest benevolence. Of course, this hostility to Christianity was not explicit nor conscious on the part of Adam Smith and his school; they were humane and devout men; it is not the intent of their teaching, it is the logic of their doctrine, that I am talking about. This same idea, says Toynbee, though nowhere stated in the writings of Ricardo, underlies them all; it is the substratum

[1] *Ency. Brit.* xix. p. 366.

on which they all rest. And the next great name of this school of economists, Malthus, puts it into language which no man can misunderstand. "The great Author of nature," he says, "with that wisdom which is apparent in all his works," has made "the passion of self love beyond comparison stronger than the passion of benevolence." If this is true, then when Christ bids us love our neighbors as ourselves, he bids us violate the law of our nature as God made it in the beginning. "By this wise provision," Malthus continues (that is, by making the passion of self-love beyond comparison stronger than the passion of benevolence), "the most ignorant are led to promote the general happiness, an end which they would have totally failed to attain if the moving principle of their conduct had been benevolence. Benevolence, indeed, as the great and constant source of action, would require the most perfect knowledge of causes and effects, and therefore can only be the attribute of the Deity. In a being so short-sighted as man, it would lead into the grossest errors, and soon transform the fair and cultivated soil of civilized society into a dreary scene of want and confusion."[1] It is true, Malthus goes on to say, that benevolence has very important uses in our social life: it is "the kind corrector of the evils arising from the other stronger passion;" it is "the balm and consolation and grace of human life, the source of our noblest efforts in the cause

[1] *Essay of Population*, edition of 1872, p. 492.

of virtue, and of our purest and most refined pleasures." Nevertheless, it is a principle wholly subordinate to self-love, and the Creator meant that it should be. In his original uprightness, man was supremely egoistic; perhaps the fall took place when good-will began to prevail over greed. Malthus does not mention it, but it is possible that his theory may offer us a new interpretation of the Adamic allegory. May it not be that the benevolence involved in the act of the woman, when she gave of the fruit of the tree to the man instead of eating it all herself, was what brought death into the world, and all our woes? It is true that Malthus wishes to have the duty of benevolence constantly enforced upon men; but how much weight such exhortations would have upon his hearers, after he had told them that the Creator "has enjoined every man to pursue as his primary object his own safety and happiness," we may easily calculate. If God has purposely made self-love incomparably stronger than benevolence in each man's nature, and if the design of this is to promote the welfare of all men, it is certainly the bounden duty of each to fulfill his Maker's design concerning himself, and to love himself supremely, and take little thought for his neighbor. It would be hard to realize that this was not a travesty, if we had not for three quarters of a century been reaping the bitter fruits of this poisonous sowing in the lives of millions. The natural man receives doctrine of this sort without cavil; it justifies and almost glorifies his strongest passion. We cannot wonder that the theories of this school obtained wide currency.

Malthus was a clergyman. How he adjusted his theories to the law of Christ I do not know. Where he could have found words by which a more flat repudiation of the second great commandment of the law could be expressed I cannot tell. No infidel since the days of Celsus has more daringly disputed the word of the Lord. Malthus was neither an evil-minded nor an impious man; there was no intention of blasphemous denial; he was simply the victim of a theory. The wonder is that he never perceived the fact that his maxims gave the lie to that which is most central and fundamental in the teachings of his Master.

Undesigned though it undoubtedly was, the effect of all these economic reasonings, in which the beneficence of an unbridled egoism is asserted or assumed, has been for a century insidiously, but none the less actively, antagonistic to Christianity, an unswerving obstacle to the progress of the Christian church, a mighty hindrance to the coming of the kingdom of heaven. No deadlier influence has been arrayed against the Christian religion; more than all the skepticism of rationalists and critics of the Scriptures, this doctrine has undermined the faith of the church and paralyzed its life. For this was a philosophy which everybody could understand, and which quickly found its way to everybody's lips. It requires no erudition to know what is meant by pursuing our own interest exclusively, in all our exchanges of services and commodities; it is the very thing we are most inclined to do; and when the great masters of economic science tell us that this is the true and only way to promote the general welfare, why should we not give free rein to our cupidity, and plunge into these fierce competitions with all our powers?

There is, of course, a basis of truth under the speculations of the old economists. It is true that God does know how to make the wrath of man and the cupidity of man to praise him; it is true that he is able to neutralize the evil effects wrought by human selfishness, and that when men pursue their own interests exclusively they are often, by the very constitution of society, forced to confer benefits upon their fellow-men. But this is a very different doctrine from that of Malthus, which we have been considering. The Ruler of the universe is so wise and so strong that he overrules human perverseness, and brings many blessings to earth, even when men disobey his laws and fight against him; but this gives us no token of the good that might be ours, if men would only obey his laws and work together with him.

The error of the old economists was an overstrained optimism. Such was not the faith of their followers. Optimism soon gave place to fatalism. The doctrine taught by later philosophers not a few was that these great movements of the economic realm were wholly outside the moral order.

"All that we can affirm with certainty," says one economist, "is that social phenomena are subject to law, and that natural laws of the social order are in their entire character like the laws of physics." This is the theory maintained by many modern writers. This whole realm, they insist, is governed by "the cold inflexible laws of supply and demand." No power on earth can change the results which naturally flow from the action of these laws. These teachers do not say with Adam Smith and Malthus that these results are always beneficent, but they say that no selfish intent of ours can make them less beneficent, and no good-will of ours can make them more beneficent, than they naturally are. It is all one, so far as the outcome is concerned, whether we are supremely selfish or disinterestedly benevolent in our conduct of business. All is included in a network of inexorable law; individual choices cannot alter the results. We may wish as employers to consider the interests of our workmen, but no kindness of ours will avail them anything; the cold inexorable laws of supply and demand have fixed their remuneration, and it is useless for us to mix sentiment of any sort with our business; it can do them no good.

It is evident that this doctrine is not any more friendly to Christian ethics than the one which it has superseded. Christian morality assumes that the wills of men are free, and that their social conditions are largely dependent on their own choices. It regards society as improvable by moral instrumentalities; it bids us pray that the kingdom of God may come, and work for the answering of our prayers. The notion that "natural laws of the social order are in their entire character like the laws of physics" is the very antithesis of the Christian morality. The effect of this doctrine upon the conduct of men must be, of course, to discourage obedience to the Christian law throughout the whole realm of industry and exchange.

The rapid growth of that unsocial and destructive mercantilism whose devastations President White so vividly described in his little tract entitled "A Century's Message" is thus pretty clearly explained. The natural love of gain is not wholly accountable for it; that master passion of humanity has been stimulated and intensified by a bad social philosophy. The egoistic impulses are strong enough in themselves; the Christian law recognizes them and uses them, counteracting them with the altruistic motives; but the prevailing social philosophy has met the Christian morality upon the very threshold of the kingdom of exchanges, and has ordered it out and barred the door against it, insisting that love has no standing-room within this realm, that self-interest is the only motive that can rationally rule in industry and trade.

A natural result of the exclusion of Christian ethics from this domain has been the weakening of its authority in every other realm. Conduct is three fourths of life, we are told; and the conduct which has to do, in one way or another, with economic questions is a large fraction of that fraction. In buying and selling, in exchanging commodities or services, in working or in directing the labor of others, most of the time of most of our neighbors is spent. In a highly organized society like ours, economic relations are found underlying and conditioning almost everything we do. If over all this part of our lives the Christian law has no control, if industry and business are beyond Christ's jurisdiction, really not much is left to him. In the minds of those who believe this, he must suffer a serious loss of respect. What sort of a King of men is he who is powerless to control the largest and intensest part of their activity? Under such limitations, the Christian vocation becomes largely a matter of sentiment; what wonder that it is handed over to women and children? We shall never win for our Master the allegiance of the strong men of this world until we show them that he has the power and the purpose to rule the shop and the factory and the counting-room as well as the church and the home.

It is evident, then, that the Christian teacher who is faithful to his commission will be brought continually into direct and uncompromising conflict with certain prevalent dogmas and influences of the old political economy. A good many other kinds of infidelity and skepticism he may very well afford to ignore; but the infidelity which plumply denies the royal law according to the Scripture, "Thou shalt love thy neighbor as thyself," which insists that this law is null and void in the largest domain of human life, is a foe with which there must be no parleying.

It is highly important, however, to take notice that the political economists of the present time are not our antagonists, but our allies, in this warfare. There are conspicuous exceptions, but the great majority of the teachers of this science now in the field repudiate the theories of which I have been speaking, and teach a doctrine in closest harmony with the Christian ethics. A great change has taken place in economic theories within the past twenty-five years. There are few colleges in this country, and scarcely any in Germany or in England, in which the traditional doctrines are now taught. The more recent works upon political economy are the arsenal from which we may furnish ourselves with the needful weapons of this warfare. But the traditional doctrines yet linger in the minds of the people; the maxims, sentiments, practices, of the average business man show how firmly they are rooted in his thought; our jurisprudence is badly infected with them; the newspaper constantly reflects them; the working classes are up in arms against them, but that is regarded as a melancholy sign of the ignorance and unreason of the working classes. The employing and trading classes learned this philosophy very quickly; it will take them longer to unlearn it. Time and patience are required to eradicate doctrines of this sort from the popular mind. Ragweed is easily propagated, but not so easily extirpated. The individualistic philosophy may be only a survival, but some curses survive very persistently.

In view of the fact that economics and ethics are so closely related, it is highly important that every Christian who tries to teach should be a careful student of this department of social science. I think that a portion of the time devoted by young theologians to mastering the heresies and controversies of the early church might usefully be given to the study of these questions which touch so nearly the moral life of the people with whom they are to deal. It is a great field, indeed; a lifetime can be spent upon it; and a smattering of knowledge picked up along its borders may easily render its possessor ridiculous, if not dangerous; nevertheless, it is imperative that the Christian pastor should exercise himself in the elements of this science. "To no class in the country," says Professor Laughlin, "does the demand for a knowledge of economic principles, and for a practical realization of the means by which the masses of men should be touched, appeal with more justice and force than to the educated ministry of the country." [1]

It may be useful to make a few practical suggestions as to the principles which should guide the Christian teacher in his application of the Christian ethics to economic questions.

[1] *The Study of Political Economy*, p. 100.

1. Let the Christian teacher get firm hold of the truth that the Christian law is a perfect and a universal law; that it applies to every form of social order; that it forms the only basis on which men can usefully and happily associate and coöperate; that it is just as applicable to industrial or commercial society as to domestic or civil society. At this point there is a vast amount of uncertainty, if not skepticism, among Christian teachers; and it is to the hesitation and timidity of their utterances respecting the nature of Christ's kingdom, and its paramount rights and claims, that a great deal of the present confusion and strife in society is due.

2. But, when they set up this claim, let them be careful to understand and not misstate the Christian law. It is not sheer altruism, — Thou shalt love thy neighbor and *not* thyself; it is the union of self-love with good-will, — Thou shalt love thy neighbor *as* thyself. It leaves room for the law of self-preservation, for the operation of a legitimate self-interest; it puts upon every man the responsibility of self-support and the obligation of self-respect; but it lifts up to equality with the self-regarding motives the motives of benevolence, putting the social duties and obligations on a par with those which the individual owes to himself. Because the man is the child of God, he has no right to neglect or despise himself; because his neighbor also is a child of the same Father, he owes to him a brother's love and care. Christianity pre-

serves, therefore, in all its force, what the economists call the individual initiative; it implies, I think, individual property. I doubt whether the character of which it furnishes the ideal could be developed in a purely communistic régime. But while it bids the man follow the natural impulse which leads him to care for himself, it evokes the other principle of benevolence, and gives it equal authority, and expects through the equivalence of these two forces to secure individual perfection and social harmony.

It is this coördination of egoism and altruism which constitutes the very kernel of the Christian ethics, and which it has seemed so very difficult for the average economist to comprehend. Malthus, evidently, could not conceive of any other condition of things except that which results from the absolute supremacy of one or the other of these two forces. In his scheme of the universe, either egoism or altruism must prevail. If self-love ruled, benevolence must be wholly subordinate; if benevolence ruled, self-love could find no room for exercise. Since he found self-love greatly in the ascendant, he inferred that this must be God's will; he thought that he was interpreting the purpose of the Creator. The Socialists, on the other hand, recoiling from the evils of excessive self-love, hail benevolence as the reigning principle of society, and refuse to give to self-love any considerable place in their reconstructed social order. These theories are both wrong; the Christian law, which makes neither of these principles supreme, which coördinates and balances them, will be found to furnish the only safe basis of social organization.

Undoubtedly it is a difficult matter to keep these forces in equilibrium. Practical morality is always a difficult matter. To find the right and follow it takes care and patience and strenuous endeavor. Selfishness is very simple; so is sentimentalism; right conduct sets for us many intricate problems. To refer all human action to one motive makes the calculation easy, but it is not always correct. The equation of the circle, with its single focus, is simpler than that of the ellipse with its two foci; but the orbits of the heavenly bodies are ellipses, nevertheless, and not circles. And when our social philosophers learn to calculate the movements of the social order according to the Christian law, with relation to these two centres of individual and social welfare, their theories will be much more useful to their fellow-men.

3. The Christian teacher must also be prepared to show, in exact contradiction to the statement of Malthus, that the general happiness is not promoted when the passion of self-love is "beyond comparison stronger than the passion of benevolence." It should not be difficult to furnish historical evidence in disproof of this monstrous assertion. Even if it could be shown that unbridled individualism will result in the most rapid production of material wealth, that does not quite prove that it is the surest path to the "general happi-

ness." The widespread discontent and social degradation which accompany this sudden increase of wealth, and the evils that threaten the overthrow of the existing order, must also be taken into the account. But, furthermore, it may be useful to make it plain, by deductive reasoning, as Mr. Sidgwick has done in his admirable chapter on "The System of Natural Liberty in Relation to Production," that the free pursuit by individuals of their own exclusive interest will not lead to universal welfare. By the same deductive process which led Bastiat into his miraculous harmonies, Mr. Sidgwick, a much finer logician, shows that "the scientific ideal of political economists cannot legitimately be taken as the practical ideal of the Art of Political Economy; since it is shown by the same kind of abstract reasoning to be liable to fail, in various ways and to an indefinite extent, of realizing the most economical and effective organization of industry."[1] The confidence of our modern *bourgeoisie* in the beneficence of sheer individualism is so strong that some pains must be taken to show them that the theory on which they are resting lacks even speculative foundations.

4. We must be able, also, to challenge the materialistic fatalism that lurks in much of our modern sociology. We must have the power to see and to show that what men call the social and economic laws are not all "inexorable;" that they are not of the character of physical laws at all;

[1] *Principles of Political Economy*, Book III. chap. ii.

that the intelligence, the conscience, and the will of man are constant elements of these social forces; that they are modifiable, therefore, by human choice and effort. These economic laws, or some of them, arise out of human nature. "But human nature," as Arnold Toynbee has said, "is not always the same. It slowly changes, and is modified by higher ideals and wider and deeper conceptions of justice. Men have forgotten that, though it is impossible to change the nature of a stone or a rock, human nature is pliable, and pliable above all to nobler ideas and to a truer sense of justice. We have no reason to suppose that human nature as it is now will always remain the same. We have reason, on the other hand, to suppose that employers, under the influence of the wider and deeper conceptions of which I have spoken, may be willing to forego, in the struggle for division of wealth, some part of that share which would come to them if they chose to exert their force without restraint. It may be said, 'This is chimerical; human nature will be the same, and always has been the same.' This I deny, and I instance that great change of opinion which took place in England with regard to slavery. If such a rapid change could take place in our moral ideas within the last hundred years, do you not think it possible that in the course of another hundred years English employers and English laborers may act upon higher notions of duty and higher conceptions of citizenship than they do now?"[1]

[1] *The Industrial Revolution*, p. 175.

But not only may we hope for a steady improvement in human nature; we also know that already, in obedience to moral motives, the men of the present time are led to change their conduct upon economic questions; and that economic results are affected, very materially, by moral considerations. The presence and the pressure of ethical motives do modify the working of economic forces.

In a late essay, written in a humane and catholic temper, I find a rather sturdy protest against the intrusion of ethical considerations into the economic realm. The two sciences are wholly distinct, this essayist insists, and must not be confused. "The question what ought to be, or what we wish, must be kept clear from the question what is, if we wish for any trustworthy answer to either." "Is there any doubt," he demands, "that our sympathy with the aspirations of the working classes in their centuries of effort, or our zeal for whatever shall bring the masses of society into the full light and warmth of modern civilization, is and must always be altogether foreign to the question as to the causes which determine wages?"[1] If the essayist means that the economist's sympathies will not directly affect the causes which determine wages, his contention may be admitted. Indirectly, however, the economist's sympathy or want of sympathy has a great deal to do with this matter. But if he means that the sympathy of the people generally, and especially of the employing classes, with

[1] *Journal of Economics*, i. 24.

the laborers in their struggles, "is and must always be altogether foreign to the question as to the causes which determine wages," then his doctrine is by no means indubitable. I should say that sympathy with the laborer, and a desire for his welfare on the part of his employers and his neighbors generally, are clearly among the causes which determine wages, — causes that often operate very efficiently, and that ought to be and would be much more efficient than they are if economists had not so diligently sought to prove that they could not operate at all. The presence or the absence of this feeling of sympathy and good-will toward the laborer affects his fortunes for good or ill very materially. It affects wages directly and perceptibly. Who does not know that the determining factor in many strikes is public opinion? The question whether the men carry their point or not depends very largely on whether they have the sympathy of their neighbors. Even so purely economic an element as rent is affected considerably by public opinion. Professor Thorold Rogers asserts that rents in England have been for long periods far below the figure which they would have reached under competition. The "disreputable publicity" attending evictions has, he says, prevented English landlords from grinding the face of their tenants. The evidence which Dr. Walker has marshaled in his chapter on "What may Help the Wages Class in its Competition for the Products of Industry"[1] is abundant and convincing.

[1] *The Wages Question*, p. 345 *seq.*

It is admitted by all economists that whatever tends to increase the efficiency of labor tends to increase wages by enlarging the product to be divided between capital and labor. But, in the words of President Walker, "the greatest possibilities of industrial efficiency lie in the creation of hopefulness, self-respect, and social ambition among the laboring class."[1] These are moral qualities, but their economic effects are of the utmost importance. And the moral qualities which have this efficiency, the hopefulness, the self-respect, and the social ambition, are surely developed and stimulated in the laboring class by the manifestation to them of sympathy and good-will on the part of their employers and their neighbors.

That terrible chapter of President Walker's on "The Degradation of Labor," from which I have just quoted a sentence, shows how fatal may be the consequences of a protracted reduction of wages. Those heavenly harmonies of the enthusiastic Frenchman, which guarantee to everybody peace and plenty, do not operate at all. The loss of vigor, of hope, of moral stamina, entails a condition which perpetuates and aggravates itself. "When people are down," says Dr. Walker, "economical forces solely are more likely to keep them down, or push them lower down, than to raise them up."[2]

Well, there are a great many people in the world who are down in just this way. What is to

[1] *The Wages Question*, p. 85.
[2] *Ibid.* p. 87.

be done with them? Their wages are very low, and tend to diminish rather than to increase. If sympathy and good-will have no place in the solution of such problems, it will surely go hard with these poor people. The fact is that it is only by the active intervention of moral agencies that such calamities can be prevented, and such injuries repaired, and such degraded masses lifted up. "Moral and intellectual causes only," says Dr. Walker, "can repair any portion of the loss and waste occasioned."

In England, for many years, factory labor suffered such a degradation as has just been described. Large masses of laborers sank, under the operation of "purely economic laws," into a condition from which they could never have risen. The sympathy and good-will of their neighbors, their rich and high-born neighbors, devised the factory legislation which rescued them from this degradation. It will scarcely be disputed that this factory legislation rescued and raised up multitudes of these hapless people; helped them to stand; enabled them to regain the ground they had lost; qualified them to earn better wages, and actually put them in possession of better wages. It would seem, then, that considerations of humanity are not necessarily altogether foreign to the question of the causes which determine wages."

This essayist insists that "the process adopted for the elucidation of scientific law must of logical necessity be kept free from ethical considerations."[1] In the name of common sense and common humanity, how can this question — the wages question — be discussed without reference to ethical considerations? The effects that we read off and tabulate as economical are in large measure due to moral causes. "No action," says a recent writer, "can be regarded as merely economic and as possessing no moral character. If I buy a coat, there are many moral questions involved; and the attendant circumstances in any actual instance will render an apparently indifferent action right or wrong. It is right to be suitably attired, and wrong to be extravagant; it is right to pay your bills punctually, and wrong to run into debt; buying a coat may in itself be either right or wrong, but in each particular case it must be one or the other; it cannot be destitute of all moral quality. Just as we cannot distinguish matters of general interest from those that are merely private, because all the affairs of citizens are indirectly of general concern, so we cannot distinguish the moral from the merely economic, because all economic conduct has moral aspects."[2]

In another part of the same periodical from which I have been quoting is a translation of a recent review by the greatest living German economist, Adolph Wagner. In this review, Wagner mentions five double motives which govern men in their economic conduct: (1) one's own industrial

[1] Quoted by *Journal of Economics*, p. 26.

[2] *Politics and Economics*, by W. Cunningham, p. 147.

advantage and the fear of want; (2) the fear of punishment and the hope of approval; (3) the sense of honor and the fear of disgrace: (4) the impulse to activity and the fear of the results of inactivity; (5) *the sense of duty and the fear of conscience.* And he insists that economic theory, "so far as it operates with psychological motives, makes deductions from them, and tries to explain phenomena that are based on economic activity, *must begin by considering the possible influence of all these motives.*"[1] The sense of duty is an economic motive, says this great economist. "We may be thankful," he goes on, "that it can appear, and does appear, in industrial actions, repressing and modifying other motives. Because of it, competition is not pressed to the utmost, prices do not reach the highest or lowest limits which the pursuit of individual advantage would fix. . . . Under this head we are to class not only all charitable action, but the cases where an industrial or social superior purposely refrains from making his own interest the exclusive ground of his economic conduct;"[2] when he acts like a Christian, that is to say, instead of an "economic man."

With such authority as this at our back, we may stand without much diffidence in the presence of the materialistic economists, and utter our protest against an economic method which carefully rules out all ethical considerations. The

[1] Quoted in *Journal of Economics*, i. 118, 122.

[2] *Ibid.* p. 121.

trouble with such an alleged science is not only that it is immoral, but that it is unscientific. Its facts are mutilated in the handling, and its causes are not true causes. Its scientific propagandists are not, happily, very numerous just now; but its disciples and devotees are a great multitude. To convert them from the error of their opinions; to make them see that right thought and kind feeling and just action are true and mighty economic forces, and that men of good-will have the power to make this, in every way, a better world to live in, is part of the work of the Christian teacher.

5. Finally, let us always insist that the increase of the national wealth, with which political economy sometimes supposes itself to be solely concerned, is subordinate to the national welfare, but is conditional for it and inseparable from it. It would be idle, of course, to give time to the study of the methods of increasing the national wealth, unless the increase of the national wealth were a thing to be desired. That is the postulate which underlies the study of economics. But the increase of the national wealth is a thing to be desired only so far as it promotes the national welfare. It will not do to assume, as many economists seem to do, that all additions to the wealth of the nation are necessarily additions to its welfare. The aggregate of material possessions may be increasing while the general well-being is suffering serious losses. The total wealth of Rome was never increasing so rapidly as in the day of the

nation's swiftest decline. To study the problems of national wealth, and keep our eyes shut to the effect produced by this wealth upon the national life, would be highly unprofitable business. The attempt to ignore this question would be demoralizing. *The methods by which this wealth is produced and distributed are acting directly and powerfully upon the character of the whole people.* The only interest that any Christian or any patriot can have in the study of these methods centres in these estimates of national character. The one question that he is concerned to ask is how this wealth and these ways of getting it are affecting the health, the vigor, the morals of the people. These material gains are means to an end, and that end is the life of the nation. It is not chiefly by the use of wealth, after it is gained, that character is affected; it is *rather in the very act of producing and exchanging it that the moral life of the individual or the community is enriched or impoverished.* How, then, can these great movements of the industrial realm ever, in any sound thinking, be dissociated from the moral issues toward which they are tending? Economics without ethics is a mutilated science, — the play of Hamlet without Hamlet. It is the work of the Christian moralist to bring together and hold together firmly, in all his teaching, what God has joined together, and what men have so long been trying to keep asunder. If those who are charged with the duty of enforcing Christian morality are faithful to their high calling, we shall see before the end of another generation a much sounder and more humane public opinion on economic questions taking the place of the conscienceless theories that have so long prevailed ; we shall see the kingdoms of industry and trade submitting themselves, as they do not now, to the law of the kingdom of heaven ; and we shall be conscious that a great hindrance to the progress of this kingdom has been taken out of the way.

III.

PROPERTY IN LAND.

THE possession of property is the one object of desire most nearly universal in civilized communities. There is no stronger passion; it exists in different degrees of development in different individuals and in different communities, but there are few who will not confess some personal experience of its cravings. "It is not," says one, "merely the love of self and wife and child that intensifies the desire for property, but the love of power in all its forms; the love of liberty and independence; and very particularly fear, — the fear of the uncertain morrow, with all its danger for the propertiless. All these and other passions and desires combine to strengthen the passion for property to an intense extreme, and even boundless degree. . . . Our moralist Carlyle vents scornful sarcasm on the English people 'whose hell is want of money or failure to make money.' I venture to affirm, on the contrary, that the hell in question, if only the poverty or lack of money is sufficiently absolute, will be, for most people, a very serious and most real hell."[1]

[1] *The Social Problem*, by William Graham, pp. 333, 335.

Since this passion is so nearly universal and so intense, it is evident that in our work as Christian witnesses we shall constantly encounter it; that it will mightily affect for good or ill the characters of the men to whom we are sent with the gospel; that no small part of our care will be the direction or the repression of this omnipresent force. It is of the utmost consequence, then, that we understand it. The institution of property, its origin in human nature, its relation to human history, its place and function in human society, is a theme that demands our patient study. What is the Christian law of property? On what basis do property rights rest in a christianized community? At any time such questions as these are of the greatest interest to him who seeks to build on the earth the kingdom of heaven, but there has been no day within the lifetime of any of us when they were pressing on the thought of men as they are to-day.

We are living under a régime of private property. The vast wealth that this teeming civilization has brought forth is nearly all in the hands of individual owners. There are government buildings here and there, on land held by the state; there are a few ships and lighthouses, with many highways and harbors, all of which are the property of the government, common property; there are parks and museums, schools and libraries, and a few colleges, owned by the community; but the great mass of all that the land brings forth, and the railways and the ships carry, and the factories transform, and the merchants distribute, is individual property. Combinations of individuals, called companies or corporations, hold much of this wealth, but this form of ownership is only a modification or extension of private ownership; the rights of the individual in all these combinations are more or less sharply discriminated.

Of private property there are many kinds, but these may be divided into three principal classes: (1) lands, including mines; (2) the products of human labor; (3) rights of future possession. Most of the land in this country is the property of individuals; the same is true of the houses, the stores, the factories, the fruits of the earth, the products of the mines and the machines, the goods and wares of every description. The silver dollar in your pocket is the product of labor, and its value is due, not wholly, but largely, to the labor which it cost to produce it. The bank-bill, however, which keeps the dollar company, owes its principal value, not to the labor expended in producing it, but to the fact that it is the sign or evidence of a right which you have acquired to the possession of five dollars' worth of gold or silver or goods of any sort for which you may wish to exchange it. You may describe it as incorporeal property, since it is not the paper of which it is composed, but the promise printed on the paper, that makes it valuable. Such are all notes, bonds, mortgages, stock certificates, patents, copyrights, and the like; they are rights, not things. Much of the property of the present day is incorporeal property; it consists of legal rights of this nature.

In a rude state of society, property of this sort does not exist to any extent; it is the creature of law; it is the instrument of a highly complex civilization. Property rights in land and in the things that have been produced by labor are also carefully *defined* by law; there is nothing that men claim as property that law does not recognize and protect. So intimate is the dependence of property upon law, in modern civilization, that some philosophers have regarded all property as the creature of law. So Bentham: "Property and law were born together, and will die together; before law there was no property; take away the law and all property ceases." This is but an echo of Montesquieu, who had written: "As men renounced their natural independence to live under political laws, they have renounced their natural community of possession to live under civil laws. The political laws give them liberty, the civil laws property." [1] The truth in this is that law is the safeguard and bulwark of property, and that property rights would be insecure and possessions meagre were it not for the protection of the laws. But it is hardly true to say that there would be no property but for law. If all the laws of the land were abrogated to-morrow, the goods in my hands, which I have earned by honest labor, would still be my property. I

[1] Lalor's *Cyclopedia*, iii. 392.

should have the same right to them that I have to-day, though I might find it difficult to maintain my right.

The incorporeal property of which I have spoken, bank-notes, bonds, stocks, and the like, is of value because it is exchangeable for commodities. The bank-note gives me a right to a specified amount of gold or silver coin; and the gold or silver coin is the common representative of exchangeable commodities. But these material commodities which I may wish to procure, all of them come forth from the earth. No man could produce them and possess them unless he had somehow acquired a right to appropriate the fruits of the earth.

You go out in the morning, with your basket on your arm and a dollar in your pocket, to the city market. This dollar of yours, where did you get it? Let us suppose that you earned it by a half-day's labor, sawing wood or plowing corn. You gave for it a fair equivalent of service. If the man who gave you the dollar got it rightfully, then you have a perfect right to it. We will not try to trace the origin of the dollar now; we assume that your right to it is perfect. You find a marketman with a load of potatoes, and proceed to exchange a part of your dollar for a portion of his load. But where did this marketman get these potatoes? If he stole them, he has, of course, no right to them, and cannot, by exchange for your money, make you their rightful possessor. "But he did not steal them," you say. "He raised them in his own garden.

They are the product of his labor." Yes, of his labor, and of the soil in which they grew. His labor was one factor of the product, the land was another. Let us admit that he is entitled to so much of the value of the product as is due to his own labor; but where did he get the right to appropriate the powers of the soil, and to make you pay him for their contribution? Now, we shall find upon analysis that as all the commodities we value come from the earth, the rights of property in them involve the right of access to the materials furnished by the earth and of labor upon them. All property in things depends on the right to use the earth. In a régime of private property, the foundation of property rights is private property in land. This may not be necessarily true, but it is historically true. Private property in the products of labor might, no doubt, coexist with common property in land; but, in the existing order, all our rights of possession are conditioned upon the possession of the earth. The farmer, the planter, the miner, the quarryman, the lumberman, go directly to the land for their goods; the mechanic and the manufacturer reshape and transform the products of the land; the merchant exchanges, and the common carrier transports, the commodities thus produced; the artisan or the laborer, the artist or the author or the parson, cannot work unless he can buy or hire a spot on the earth's surface to stand upon while he labors. The need of land and of its products is the fundamental need of human beings; the right of access to the land, of a share in its bounty, of a standing-place upon it, must, then, be among our fundamental rights. It is no more true that the land is the foundation of all our edifices than that a right to the land is the foundation of all our property rights. Nevertheless, we do not find all men in possession of this right. In Great Britain, only about one person in thirty-five owns any land; not one in a hundred owns any cultivated land. In this country, the number of landed proprietors, though much larger in proportion, is still much less than the total population, and much less even than the number of families. The greater part of the people in this country are, and will always be, landless.

How, then, did those who are now in possession of the land acquire their title to it? If you have a house-lot or a farm to which you can show a clear claim, you obtained it, perhaps, by purchase; the man of whom you purchased it transferred to you his title; the man of whom he purchased it transferred the title to him: thus, by a series of fair contracts and legal transfers, the land has come down to you from the first proprietor. Your title is therefore as good as that of the first proprietor. But how did this first proprietor acquire his right?

I will not weary you with any extended criticism of the various theories of property which the jurists and philosophers have propounded; I will merely refer to them. The theory of Savigny and Blackstone makes occupancy, matured by prescription, the foundation of property rights. According to this theory, he who takes the land, and holds it for a certain number of years, has the right to it. This founds the right on force, which may answer the purposes of law, but is an ethical solecism. You can no more get right out of force than you can gather grapes from a bramble bush.

Locke counted the land as originally valueless, and made its value consist in the results of the labor expended upon it. The man who first cultivated it gained a right to it by his labor. It is very far from being true, however, that land has no value until labor is expended upon it; and while the first cultivator might be entitled to the fruits of his labor, and to any improvement in the land resulting from his labor, it is hard to understand how the fact of his working on the land gives him a perpetual and exclusive title to the land itself.

Another theory makes property simply the extension and completion of the rights of life and liberty. If a man has a right to live, he has a right to seek and to own that by which life is supported. He has, therefore, a right to occupy the earth and to cultivate it; he has a right to a dwelling-place upon the planet, and to such portions of the earth's bounty as he may be able to take for himself without interfering with the rights of others. All this may be admitted; nevertheless, it does not clearly appear what right a man could thus acquire to the exclusive and permanent possession of any portion of the earth's surface. This theory would seem to justify common property in land, rather than private property.

This fact of common property is, indeed, the fact which confronts us whenever we extend our studies into the primitive forms of social life. The philosophers have generally started with the assumption of a lone individual, landing on an island or discovering a continent, and have proceeded to derive their theories of property from his relations to the land and to the people who came after him. They have taken it for granted that the individualistic régime was the earliest form of social organization, — a society composed of individuals, each possessing definite and exclusive property rights. But the historical fact is, that the present system of individual property was preceded by a communistic system.

"So far as history speaks with any confidence on the matter," says Professor Graham, "she shows us man at first, but still late in his career, in a community, with goods in common. The group or clan is assumed to have a common origin or ancestry, and the community of blood has carried with it community of property. There is no such thing as individual property, and the conception, 'This is mine,' would scarcely rise in the minds of any members, save, perhaps, in a vague way in the mind of the chief or head, who, we find, is sometimes spoken of in the records as the owner of all the property of the family, and if not also of all the persons composing it, at least of the slaves, that invariable adjunct of early patriarchal communities. But this is but a mode of speech, the ideas connoted by which differed even very considerably from those which we would attach to them. The reality was that property belonged to all, and only such portions of it as food became the momentary property of individuals, for their use, but not for their appropriation or accumulation. Even their food was not property, in one sense. It was apportioned out under the direction of the head, who was merely the administrator. It was not his to give or to keep, and it only became the property of the recipient in a very narrow sense. It was his only if he used it, and only to the extent of his use; otherwise, it reverted to the common stock and store, and so was not individual property, in one sense. Nor was it much otherwise as regarded clothes and personal ornaments and arms. These were not at first conceived as the property of the wearers, but rather as something belonging to all and lent out to the individuals, which reverted to the community at their death." [1]

The political science deduced by Rousseau and his tribe from their own consciousness, in which the noble savage is represented as roaming alone through the woods, and finally settling on some spot of the earth's surface, and there developing himself into a first-class political integer, with all his rights and powers and perquisites and properties about him, — thus armed and equipped, en-

[1] *The Social Problem*, pp. 292–3.

tering into contract with certain other equally endowed political integers to form a political association, in which each one agrees to surrender or hold in abeyance a certain portion of his individual rights, — is purely imaginary. "Rousseau," as one has said, "invented the 'social contract,' to which the objection exists that it was invented by Rousseau, and never entered into by man."[1] The historical studies of scholars like Maine, McLennan, Seebohm, and Laveleye prove to us that man, so far as we know him, is a gregarious animal, and that his earliest appearance in history is not as a solitary, but as the member of a community in which the property is held in common, and the welfare of each is the interest of all.

Nevertheless, in those early times, we find forces at work to break up this communal life, and to introduce the régime of private property. Just how this was done we may never very accurately know; the processes of development in these primitive societies are sometimes hard to trace. Howbeit, it seems evident that this change of tenure was the result of collisions between tribes, making a military organization necessary, and thus exalting the head of the tribe or clan to a kind of supremacy that he would not have gained in the pursuits of peace. That there is a tendency in the primitive commune toward private property is true; and that the common estate would almost certainly have been broken up into individual portions by

[1] *New Social Teachings*, p. 175.

the operation of other forces, if the clan had had no battles to fight, is altogether probable. But, as a matter of fact, this change seems to have come about as the result of those intertribal wars which were so frequent and so fierce in the early days. The admirable article on "Land" in the "Encyclopædia Britannica, unsigned," but bearing some internal marks of the handiwork of Sir Henry Maine, thus traces the course of this development in ancient Germany: —

"The natural increase of population, combined with the pressure put upon the Germanic tribes from the East by the Slavs, made their territories too small for their ambition, if not for their maintenance, and five or six succeeding centuries were marked in the history of Europe chiefly by successive Germanic conquest and occupation of western and southern territory. The enormous increase of power and possession made it impossible for the original tribal government to survive; the great generals developed into kings and emperors, and their lieutenants (more or less independent according to individual capacity and distance from the capital) became dukes and counts. Gradually military authority, embracing the old idea of the land being the property of the state, evolved the new notion of feudalism. The sovereign represented the state: to him, in that capacity, land conquered from the enemy or forfeited in unsuccessful rebellion became subject; and he granted it to his followers on condition of faithful service in war. They promised to be his men, and from their own tenants they exacted in turn the like promise on the like conditions. The general insecurity made even free owners willing to buy the support of the sovereign on similar terms. Thus by degrees, less by derivation from the idea of Roman law, to which it is sometimes attributed, than by the mere necessity of the times, and as a consequence of the incessant state of warfare in which mankind existed, there came to be established the feudal doctrine that all land was held by the sovereign (on condition of suit and service), and that each immediate tenant of the sovereign was entitled to sub-infeudate his possession on the same principles. Gradually, the further attributes of property were added; service in war was commuted into rents and the peaceful service of tilling the lord's reserved domain. The right of hereditary succession became grafted on the personal grant; the power of sale and devise followed. Local usages still had influence; but it may be said broadly that from about the tenth century private property, subject to feudal conditions, became the principle of the tenure of land in Europe." [1]

This seems to be the way in which private property in land came to exist. War made the chief the supreme dictator, the king or the emperor. With the sovereignty went the domain. The land was the state's; the king became the state; then the land was the king's. He parceled it out among

[1] Vol. xiv. p. 262.

his retainers, on condition of military service, and they among theirs on like conditions. Gradually, military service was exchanged for rent, and the tenant's right became hereditary and transferable. Thus the land, which originally was the common property of the whole community, became the property of certain individuals, a small minority of the community. For these feudal proprietors, great and small, were few in comparison to the whole community. The serfs and the slaves, who tilled the lands, but had no property in them, constituted the great mass of the people.

When the era of discovery began, the new lands were claimed for his monarch by every loyal discoverer. The soil of North America was thus the subject of dispute among the European sovereigns. Henry VIII. supposed himself to be the proprietor of a large share of this continent; the title had been won for him by the brave sailors of the realm. His claim was not, of course, conceded by the Spanish monarchs. When John Cabot and his son set sail in search of the western world, they bore a patent from the seventh Henry, "empowering them to seek out, subdue, and occupy, at their own charges, any regions which before had 'been unknown to all Christians.' They were authorized to set up the royal banner and possess the territories discovered by them as the king's vassals." [1] The feudal principle was thus distinctly asserted in all the occupation by Europeans of American soil.

[1] Art. "Cabot," *Ency. Brit.* iv. 622.

Our fathers took the soil of New England and of Virginia on these terms. A patent from the king gave them all the rights they had. He had gained it by discovery, and held it as lord paramount; they held under him.

Such, then, is the historical origin of private property in land. Yet, doubtless, from the beginning, the individualistic régime was pretty sure to come. The communistic society lacked the elements of vigor and enterprise; it could not work out the problems before the race; it could not achieve the progress in the material arts for which humanity was destined; it must have made way at some time, under some sort of pressure, for the institution of private property, even if war had not created the feudal hierarchy. Human nature being what it was in those early times, the land would be more diligently cultivated and would bring forth larger harvests if it were tilled by those who had a permanent interest in its cultivation and improvement. The man who was allowed to have a piece of land to himself, subject only to necessary charges for the public good, and to keep for himself and his family what he could raise upon it, or to exchange his products for the products of his neighbors, would work harder and produce more than the man who toiled only to replenish the stores of the commune, and obtained nothing out of those stores but a bare livelihood. The idle and the thriftless would, indeed, be better off under the commune; but the industrious and the enterprising would be worse off. The industrious and the enterprising would discover that fact, at length, and would demand a reorganization of society, under which their industry and enterprise might reap their natural reward. And these classes are apt to have things their own way; it is not the idle and the thriftless that history consults when she shapes the great movements of the social order.

Nevertheless, if this change had been made from common property to private property by peaceful instead of warlike methods, it could only have been made rightfully on the ground of the public welfare. The community would never have yielded its possession of the land to individuals if it had not believed that it — the community — would be the gainer by the change. It could never have meant to surrender its paramount right to the land; it would have allowed this distribution among individuals only tentatively, and with many qualifications. "For certain purposes, and under certain restrictions," it must have said to those who received these titles, "you may retain possession of this land, and may convey your right in it by sale or bequest; but the community still retains the supreme right to the domain which it occupies, and it will resume its control over this domain, or any portion of it, whenever the public welfare shall require it. It allows these individual possessions for the promotion of the good of all; whenever it becomes evident that the good of all is not promoted by individual property in land, that institution will be abolished, and the land will again be common property."

The notion, then, that property in land is something peculiarly sacred and indefeasible, that it is a right which the state cannot touch, that every interference with landed property is spoliation and piracy, has no basis in history or reason. Few modern jurists would give this notion any countenance. That writer in the "Encyclopædia Britannica" from whom I have before quoted declares that those who hold this extreme view "show entire ignorance of the history of land tenure at all times." "Nor is there any theory of the basis of property," he continues, "which does not tacitly admit that it is subject to the authority of the community. If derived from occupation, it owes its title to the agreement of the community to support that title. If derived from labor, it is valid only for the life of the laborer, and whoever succeeds to him must take it, not as a gift from a dead man, whose rights end with the grave, but as a gift from the state, which deems that there is advantage in encouraging labor by the certainty of transmitting its produce. In every view it must be admitted that the state, by whose regulations and force property is maintained, must have an unqualified right to prescribe the conditions under which it will confer its gifts on private individuals."[1]

I have traced with some care the historical origin

[1] Vol. xiv. p. 266.

of private property in land in order to show that that extremely individualistic view which has colored much of our political philosophy is not at all tenable. Those replies to Mr. Henry George which consist of hysterical outcries of amazement that any one could dare to touch, in the name of the state, a vested interest so sacred as that of the freeholder are quite beside the mark. The soundest jurisprudence makes the right of the state superior to the right of any private proprietor. The land is held by the state for the benefit of the whole people, and the right of private proprietors cannot be allowed to override or obstruct the rights of the whole people. The moment it can be made to appear that the welfare of the whole people would be promoted by the resumption of the control of the land by the state, that moment the abolition of private property in land will be a political necessity. Compensation to individual owners would, of course, be equitable and imperative; but no supposed sacredness of individual tenure could divest the people of any nation of their supreme right to the national domain. President Walker has disputed Mr. Henry George quite as stoutly as any one; yet he says that the system of private property in land "sacrifices, at the very beginning, the equities of the subject-matter."[1] It is not on the ground of equity, but solely as a matter of political and economic expediency, he declares, that private property in land has been permitted.

[1] "Socialism," *Scribner's Magazine*, i. 118.

It is quite worth while to go on to the bottom of these questions of property rights, because they are questions that may, very likely, be hotly discussed during the next twenty-five years, and the Christian moralist will need to have clear ideas concerning them. And he will be greatly interested in knowing that the conclusion reached by the historical philosophers and jurists, although it is quite in conflict with the current individualism, is in perfect harmony with the Christian doctrine of property. When he intelligently sets forth the teachings of the Bible respecting property rights, he will find himself declaring a doctrine to which Maine and Bluntschli and Laveleye give their heartiest assent. What, then, for substance, is the Christian doctrine of property in land?

The Christian doctrine of property in land depends upon the Christian doctrine of the Nation. That doctrine, which has been stated with so much power by Dr. Mulford, is briefly this: that the Nation is a body of men inhabiting, continuously, a certain territory, held together by certain historic relationships and sympathies, having a common spirit and purpose, organized for moral ends, and holding its charter from God himself. "The sovereignty of the Nation," says Mulford, "is from God and of the people." [1] "The people, holding their authority from God," says Brownson, "hold it not as an inherent right, but as a trust from him, and are accountable to him for it. It is not

[1] *The Nation*, p. 53.

their own." [1] To the Nation thus constituted a domain is given. If God gives the Nation a right to live, he must give it a place to live. The earth is the Lord's, and the fullness thereof; he is the only absolute proprietor; but he intrusts to the Nation, for its use, the soil on which it lives, and holds the Nation responsible for the right use of it. "The right to the land is in the people," says Dr. Mulford, "and the land is given to the people in the fulfillment of a moral order on the earth. . . . The land in its integral unity is thus a divine gift, a habitation of the people for all generations. It shares in the sacredness of the life of the Nation; historical associations grow up around it, and blended with their traditions it passes sacredly from the fathers to the children, and constitutes in its wide domain the heritage and the homestead of the people." [2]

The Nation, thus ordained by God, and intrusted by him with a portion of the earth's surface as its domain and treasure-house, exists in the earth for the fulfillment of the divine purpose, for the establishment here of righteousness and peace, for the maintenance of freedom and order, for the building up of the kingdom of heaven. The end which it must seek is not the welfare of certain favored classes, but the welfare of all, — the physical, intellectual, and moral welfare of the whole people. In the distribution of its land among its citizens,

[1] *The American Republic*, p. 127.
[2] *The Nation*, pp. 65–71.

this is the principle by which it must always be guided. "As the land is the possession of the people," says Dr. Mulford, "it cannot be held as the patrimony of a prince or the monopoly of a class. The land belongs to the people constituted as a Nation; and the right to it is in its moral order. The exclusive possession and entail of the whole domain by a few may prevent and subvert the moral order, as it destroys, for instance, the life of the family. In England there are those which are called great families, but as its homes are swept away the family life of the whole people is destroyed."[1] Against such a distribution of the national domain as that which now exists in England Christian morality protests: that nation has not been administering its trust in the interest of the whole people; the monopoly of land which it has permitted is unjust and oppressive; it cannot rightfully suffer hundreds of thousands of acres to be shut up in parks and pleasure grounds and game preserves, while millions of its poor are hungry and homeless.

There is some reason to fear that we of the United States are no longer entitled, on this score, to throw stones at England. The manner in which we have permitted our own national domain to be alienated and monopolized indicates that the people of this country have not been awake to their highest responsibilities. At least one hundred and twenty-five millions of acres of the most fertile

[1] *The Nation*, p. 6.

lands of the country have been made over to various great railroad corporations. These vast tracts, equal to four or five States of the size of Ohio, in extent more than twice the whole of New England, enough to make forty Connecticuts, have been committed, without reserve, to these companies; and all this land may be, and much of it has been, sold in enormous quantities to speculators and monopolists. A landed aristocracy is thus rapidly growing in all the West. I find, in a recent volume, the statement that more than twenty million acres of our domain — about eight Connecticuts — are owned by foreign capitalists, in areas of not less than fifty thousand acres each. Thus the English Duke of Sutherland owns 420,000 acres of our soil; the Marquis of Tweeddale, 1,750,000 acres; Sir Edward Reid & Co., two millions of acres in Florida; a Scotch company, made up largely of the nobility, have half a million acres in the same State; a similar English company, three millions of acres in Texas.[1] To what complexion this will come anybody can see. We shall have a great number of absentee landlords holding and leasing or cultivating by agents a large part of our domain. This is an iniquity far worse than the land monopoly of Great Britain. The American people are verily guilty in that they have suffered such a power for oppression to take root in their soil. Doubtless they meant well enough, so far as they had any intent at all in the matter; their great

[1] *Labor, Land, and Law*, by W. A. Phillips, p. 357.

haste to build railroads and develop the country was the motive; but they have been culpably reckless in the disposal of their domain, and they have sown their land with dragon's teeth that may bring forth erelong an ugly harvest. Now that nearly all the arable land of the country is gone out of the control of the Nation into the hands of speculators and monopolists, we begin to see how blameworthy our negligence has been. No such state of things would now exist if the Christian law of the responsibility of the Nation for the use of the domain had been enforced, and the conscience of the people had been awakened to the magnitude of this trust. If the American people had been made to feel the solemnity of the obligation resting on them to make the right use of this vast estate intrusted to them by the Creator, as the Hebrews were made to feel their responsibility for the just distribution of the land of their little country among their people, we should have escaped some dangers that now sorely threaten us.

We may approach the Christian doctrine of property in land from the point of view of the individual as well as from that of the Nation.

The right to life is ranked in all systems of Christian ethics as the first of the rights of man. But if I have a right to live, I must also have the right to acquire and possess that which is necessary to support life. To say that one has a right to life, but no right to property, is a flat contradiction. The right to live involves the right to procure the food by which life is preserved, and this involves some rights in the soil out of which the food all comes. The state, whose business it is to protect my rights, must see to it that this right is not lost. It cannot, then, permit any such exclusive ownership of the soil by some as shall debar others from obtaining sustenance. When the soil is parceled out under a system of private ownership, and there are large numbers who are not owners of land, the right of these landless millions to life is higher and more sacred than the right of the landholders to their property.

Furthermore, my right to live obviously involves the right of standing-room on this planet. Yet if I am not the owner of any real estate, and if the doctrine of the exclusive private ownership of the soil is true, I have no such right. I am not permitted to squat in the highway; the police compel me to move on. Nowhere else have I any right. I may be able to secure of a neighbor the privilege of dwelling for a limited time on land that belongs to him; but he may refuse, and all my neighbors who own land may refuse, to rent me a spot to live upon. I live in this world, then, by the favor of those who own the land. I have no rights here. The same is true of the millions of the landless. They are all here by sufferance. If it should please the landowners to combine and order the rest of mankind into the lakes and the sea, we should be forced, by this doctrine, to go.

These logical consequences of the individualistic

theory show that it is not tenable. It is not by sufferance of the landowners that the rest of mankind are on this planet: all of us have rights here; standing-room is ours by right; a chance to earn our living here is ours by right; and the state must permit none of its citizens in any wise to abridge or obstruct these rights. *No man's right of private property in land can be so sacred as every man's right to standing-room on the face of the earth.* And in all its laws of property and its theories of land tenure, the state is bound to keep the just proportion between the more sacred and the less sacred rights.

The Christian must hold the land, then, by a very different tenure from that hard-and-fast individualism which has been prescribed by recent political science. He recognizes the fact that the land is the bounty of the Creator, committed to the Nation in trust for the people; and that it must be distributed and administered by the Nation, acting in God's stead, for the benefit of the whole people. In his own occupation of the land he will endeavor to follow this principle. He will allow himself no use of the land, and no disuse of it, that conflicts with the public good; and he will seek to have the national administration of the domain directed always toward the public good.

Does this mean Communism? Not at all. It does mean some sharp restrictions upon the monopoly of land, upon the holding of land for speculative purposes, upon the conduct of those who seek to turn the bounty of nature into a means of oppression. It means the assertion of the power of the Nation over the land; the recognition of the duty of the Nation to see that the land is administered for the public good; the prompt interference by the Nation with any misuse of it that militates against the public good. Very possibly the people may make mistakes in their attempts to regulate this matter; democracies are not infallible; but democracies must not, therefore, shirk their responsibilities. "Sustained," says Cairnes, "by some of the greatest names, — I may say by every name of the first rank in political economy, from Turgot and Adam Smith to Mill, — I hold that the land of a country presents conditions which separate it economically from the great mass of the other objects of wealth; conditions which, if they do not absolutely and under all circumstances impose upon the state the obligation of controlling private enterprise in dealing with land, at least explain why this control is in certain stages of social progress indispensable, and why, in fact, it has been constantly put in force whenever public opinion or custom has not been strong enough to do without it."[1]

It may not be necessary for the Christian teacher to discuss the methods by which the state shall administer this trust; but it may be wise, when the debate grows hot, for him to bring the broad equities and the clear obligations of the matter before

[1] Quoted by Walker, *Scribner's Magazine*, i. 118.

the minds of the people. The principle that the land is the property of the whole people, and is to be administered for their benefit, is indubitable; the question what method of administration will best secure the good of the whole people is a practical question of great difficulty. Dr. Walker says that, notwithstanding the admitted fact that the system of private property sacrifices in its very beginning the equities of the subject-matter, the advantages attending it are "so manifest, so vast, and so conspicuous" that there seems little probability that it will be superseded by state ownership. We have plenty of evidence from past ages that communal ownership did not practically secure the welfare of the people; we have evidence enough before our eyes that individualism brings forth gigantic evils. Almost certainly it will be found necessary, in the present state of society, to combine private ownership with some measure of public control, so that the gains of enterprise may not be lost, and the mischiefs of monopoly may be averted.

John Stuart Mill had a plan of appropriating for the state "the unearned increment of land." The abstract justice of this proposition is not disputed. It is manifestly unfair that a speculator should seize upon a tract of land in the neighborhood of a growing community, and simply sit on it and hold it down, — never expending a dollar in improving it, — and then, when the value has increased tenfold, or perhaps a hundredfold, by the growth of the community, enrich himself by the sale of it. The multiplied value of this land is due to nothing that he has done; it is due to the industry and enterprise of the people of the community. The gain rightfully belongs to them, and not to him. The only question is, whether it is practicable, by some system of taxation, to appropriate this unearned increment for the community. It might be found that the effort to secure this advantage would be burdensome rather than beneficial to the community. And there is another side to this question which the land reformers do not always so clearly see. There is an unearned increment; there is also an uncompensated decrement. Land in cities and towns is often sold at prices which cannot be maintained, and in the shrinkage of land values purchasers are compelled to contribute out of their hard earnings a great deal of money for the benefit of the mechanics and traders in such communities. Let us suppose the case of a man who buys for ten thousand dollars a home in some very enterprising city. At the time of his purchase real estate happens to be at the top of the wave; soon it begins to depreciate; in a few years, on his removal from the city, he is compelled to sell his home for six thousand dollars. Four thousand dollars of the money that he has earned by hard work is left behind in that community. Who has got it? It may have gone originally into the hands of real estate dealers; but it was distributed by them to carpenters, masons, painters, plumbers, and other mechanics; it tended to increase the demand for labor, and to raise the price of labor in that community; grocers and butchers and dry-goods merchants in the neighborhood got their share of it; it helped to make business brisk and the city prosperous. In the rise of real estate values the holders of real estate profit by the enterprise of the community, but in the shrinkage of real estate values the business of the community lays heavy tribute upon the savings of the holders of real estate. And there is a great deal more of this uncompensated decrement, the country through, than we are apt to take account of. If, now, it is just to take away from proprietors the unearned increment, why is it not also just to restore to them the uncompensated decrement? It is evident that this would introduce some serious practical complications. Of course it is true that in a growing country the increment exceeds the decrement; but when the other side is taken into consideration, the injustice of the present system appears much less flagrant.

It is much more likely that some modification of the laws of bequest and inheritance of land may be attempted. But that, too, is a practical matter to be settled with a view to the public good.

Difficult questions, all these, no doubt. The administration of government is a difficult business. That is not an excuse for neglecting it; it is a reason why the people, whose business it is, should give their best thought to it, and should choose their wisest men to attend to it.

We saw, a little while ago, that the earliest appearance of men in history was in communal relations. But we are not certain that we discover here the earliest form of property. This might have been a secondary stage of human development; it might have been preceded by an individualistic régime. Some animals are communists, and some are not: sheep incline to the communal order; the dog, with his bone, as Mr. Spencer says, is something of an individualist. The troglodytes of prehistoric times may have been much more like the dog with his bone than like the buffalo in his herd. The formation of the commune may have been the first social revolution. But if so, it was one of those revolutions that do not go backward. It was in the direct line of the development of the race; it was a step toward the realization of the divine purpose. When, after ages of this communal life, the institution of private property supplanted it, that in its turn was a movement forward. Men had gained by their communal life certain social qualities; they needed a training in self-reliance and enterprise; above all, they needed a development of family life, which they could not receive under communism. Great have been the benefits, unspeakable the gains wrought out for mankind under this individualistic régime. But the injuries and losses, too, have been terrible, and we are beginning to recoil from these with a reasonable fear. The indications are that the pendulum is swinging back toward a system of common property in land. Sober thinkers on both continents are discussing this possibility with patience and candor. It is not at all improbable that some of us may live to see the land of England become the property of the nation. I doubt whether any of us will live long enough to see this take place in America. The practical evils of private ownership in this country have been so few, and its obvious benefits so many, that we are not, I think, very nearly ready for Mr. George's revolution. Yet it may come, by and by. The equities and the expediencies are often far apart, but every century brings them nearer together.

It is by these zigzag lines that the human race goes forward. Possibly, after many vibrations, due to these opposing forces of individual interest and social need, mankind will learn how to coördinate them, and gain as their resultant a steady movement forward, — combining the benefits of private enterprise with the blessings of social coöperation, and realizing the divine order by loving their neighbors as themselves.

IV.

PROPERTY IN GENERAL.

THE most profound and perfect definition of property that I have ever seen is that of the Roman Catholic writer, Dr. Brownson: "Property is communion with God through the material world." The realization of this truth, and the practical application of it, would revolutionize society. The old Gnostic dualism which held matter to be essentially evil has been fatally persistent through all the Christian centuries: it was the root of monasticism; in every generation it has vitiated the theories of Puritan as well as Papist about the uses of the external world. Those who regarded material things as essentially evil could not be expected to seek or find any moral profit in the use of them. If the taint of corruption abides upon the wealth that men accumulate here, all our contact with it must be somewhat contaminating. Necessary it may be to our existence in this world, but it is a necessary evil; the less we have to do with it, the better for our souls. We must needs get property, but in having it there is harm, and in using it there is peril; the only benefit we can derive from it is that which comes through the mortification of our natural love for it when we give it away. This was the view of many of the early church Fathers. "Rightly," says Jerome, "does Jesus call wealth the unrighteous mammon, for all wealth arises from unrighteousness. The one can only gain what the other loses; hence the saying, 'Every rich man is a rogue, or the heir of a rogue.'" That thrift is permissible some of the Father's freely allow, but it is only because of the hardness of men's hearts; penury is the holier vocation. "When the right use of wealth is spoken of" by the early Fathers, says Dr. Uhlhorn, "giving it away is always dwelt on in a one-sided manner. Nay, it may be said that the Fathers see its right use in giving it away. Its use for our own necessities is, indeed, conceded, and even the adornments and enjoyments of life permitted, but still these are already under a cloud. They are not exactly sins, but they are weaknesses."[1] The seeds of communism are in all this early teaching, and the germ of that primitive communism was the ascetic feeling about property. Thus, Augustine once urges that all the trouble among men, as wars, strifes, extortions, injustices of every kind, spring from individual ownership. Over the things which we possess in common, like the sun and the atmosphere, he says, we never quarrel. "Let us, therefore, my brethren," he exhorts, "abstain from the possession of private property, or from the love of it, if we cannot abstain from the possession of it." Not

[1] *Christian Charity in the Early Church*, p. 301.

all the Fathers talk in this tone; some of the most clear and wholesome utterances on this subject in the whole range of Christian teaching are to be found in their writings. Thus Clement of Alexandria, as paraphrased by Dr. Uhlhorn, tells us that "we are not to cast away our property. It is the material, the instrument, subjected to the right use of those who know how to make a right use of it. If any one makes the wrong use of a tool, the tool is blameless. And this is the case with wealth wrongly applied as it is by many. Its nature is to be useful, and everything depends upon how it is applied." [1] Nevertheless, the prevalent sentiment of those early times regarded property as a burden to the soul, and hoped for little good from the possession of it, or from the use of it except in almsgiving. It would be easy to forecast the mischief wrought by such a sentiment. If the most fundamental and universal need of human beings is a need of that which is morally injurious, if men must be largely occupied through all their lives in getting that which they would better not possess, the case is certainly unfortunate. To say that that which is necessary to my life is hurtful to my soul is to make a grave accusation against the Author of the universe. To tell men when they go out into this wide realm of material interests, that it is all foreign to God's kingdom, a hostile sovereignty that may never be subdued to the empire of the Christ, is to give them warrant and justification for all the

[1] *Christian Charity in the Early Church*, p. 130.

evil they may be inclined to do therein. The ascetic theory of property opens the door to every kind of abuse. Who could be expected to make a right use of that which is essentially wrong?

This hoary heresy is not yet quite dead. The theory may not often find confessors, but the sentiment is still unconsciously cherished. There are not many of those engaged in the accumulation of property who do not feel that their property interests are separate from, if not contrary to, their spiritual interests. No more mischievous error could be imagined. If those concerns of a man which occupy and must occupy a large share of his life are irreligious, or even unreligious, then religion is and must be a secondary interest of his life. If he is necessarily injured, or at any rate stunted in his higher nature by getting and using money, and can only repair this injury by giving it away, it will certainly go hard with most of our neighbors.

Over against this defective and dangerous doctrine stands the wise word of the great Catholic teacher: "Property is communion with God through the material world." Let no man suppose that this is some mystical or transcendental notion; it is a statement as precise, as literal, as practical, as can be expressed in words. It is the fundamental fact on which the Christian doctrine of property is based. Until a man has comprehended it, and all that it implies, he has not fully entered into the meaning of Christian discipleship. Let us consider some of these implications.

I. This doctrine implies that God is the absolute owner of the material universe, and that we hold what we rightfully have under him. "The earth is the Lord's, and the fullness thereof; the world, and they that dwell therein." Here is the only original and absolute proprietorship. Let us not try to take this in some metaphorical or accommodated sense. There are figures of rhetoric in the Bible, but this is not one of them. It is the literal fact. The earth does belong to the Creator. There are no absolute rights of property except his rights.

But Paul says that there is a Spirit within us, a voice speaking in the secret places of our thought, and testifying to our spirits that we are the children of God. This is the deepest truth of human nature, the foundation fact of human history. It is the blessed message of the gospel which the Father of us all has been seeking, through all the generations, to bring home to human hearts. Very imperfectly have his children comprehended this great truth; the voice that was speaking in them of their divine relationships they have but faintly heard. Nevertheless, this is the portion of every one of us, though we often cast it from us, or bargain it away as Esau did for a little cheap enjoyment.

The inference which Paul draws from this fact of the divine fatherhood is a bold one, but it is inevitable: "The Spirit himself beareth witness with our spirit that we are children of God, and *if children, then heirs*." If the earth is the Lord's, and the fullness thereof, we his children and heirs possess it through our relationship to him; our rights of property are all derived from him.

The younger son in the parable claimed and received as his exclusive possession his portion of his father's estate. The heavenly Father never willingly divides his estate in this manner. It is held for all his children as one patrimony. There is enough for all, — enough for maintenance, for comfort, for enjoyment, for culture, for the highest development, for the fullest usefulness; and he desires that all his children shall have all they can use; there is no grudging distribution of the good gifts of Providence; if any one fail to receive as much as this, it is his own fault, or the fault of the other heirs; it is not through any defect in the infinite Bounty. But what any man receives of material good he takes from the hand of his heavenly Father; and he must consider the distribution as made continuously for his needs. The petition in the Lord's Prayer, "Give us this day our daily bread," is no superfluous request, even when it falls from the lips of a reputed millionaire.

It is involved in this statement that the property in my hands, be it much or little, has not been gained by despoiling my neighbor. I have not obtained it by robbery or fraud or extortion; I did not get it by taking advantage of the weakness or the ignorance or the necessity of my fellow-man, and thus coercing him to yield to me his portion.

For all that I possess, which is not the direct product of my own labor, I have striven to give a fair equivalent, in service or commodity. If property is communion or copartnership with God in the possession and use of natural things, then I can have no *property* in that which I have obtained by injustice. So far as human law is concerned, my title may be good; I may have succeeded in extinguishing the legal claim of those from whom I have unrighteously taken these possessions, for human law is but a clumsy contrivance for securing perfect justice, and often fails of its purpose. But we are not now talking about human legalities, we are talking about divine equities; and since all true property rights are based on our union with God, it is plain that we can have no property in that which we have gained by injustice. God has never been partner with us in spoliation or trickery. Of every possession thus gained, Proudhon's apothegm is true: it is robbery. But it is not property; that is the error in Proudhon's statement. Property is a word of divine significance, and we must not lightly apply it to possessions wrongfully obtained. We speak of the sacredness of property, and nothing is more sacred. Plunder is not sacred, indeed, but plunder is not property. The function of human law in this realm is to discriminate between these two: to prevent plunder and to secure property. Because those who make and administer human law are neither omniscient nor infallible, this must be very imperfectly done, but it is the ideal which jurisprudence must keep steadily in view.

Let us endeavor to realize a little more perfectly what is involved in this doctrine that property is communion with God through the material world. It implies that the material world is not essentially corrupt; it most clearly denies the old Gnostic heresy. When Jesus said, "My Father worketh hitherto," he pointed to the perpetual divine activity in nature. The first chapter of Genesis represents God as putting forth his power to prepare the material world as an abode for man, and then giving life to man, and joining man with himself in possession of the things that had been made. "And God said, Let us make man in our image, after our likeness: and let them have dominion over the fish of the sea, and over the fowl of the air, and over the cattle, and over all the earth, and over every creeping thing that creepeth upon the earth. And God created man in his own image, in the image of God created he him; male and female created he them. And God blessed them: and God said unto them, Be fruitful, and multiply, and replenish the earth, and subdue it; and have dominion over the fish of the sea, and over the fowl of the air, and over every living thing that moveth upon the earth." This may be allegory; even so, it sets forth the profoundest spiritual truth, when it shows the Creator himself at work fitting up the world for man's abode, and calling man to be partner with him in this work. It is the Creator himself who has been at work, for ages on ages, to fertilize these meadows and these prairies, to stock them with grasses and grains, to plant the great forests on the mountain sides, to store the marble and the granite and the coal and the oil and the silver and the gold in the bosom of the earth against the time of man's need. When men put forth their strength to cultivate this soil and to develop all this wonderful wealth, they are working together with God; they are thinking his thoughts after him, and moving along the line of his eternal purpose. It is strange that men should ever have deemed that in accepting the trust which God has put into their hands, and in becoming partners with him in the work that has employed him since the morning stars first sang together, they were engaging in an occupation that was essentially evil.

If, now, the production of wealth is a holy avocation, it is plain that the possession and use of it cannot be unholy. That it may be held in an unholy spirit and used for unholy ends is too evident, but this is an abuse of it; the normal method of holding and using it must be essentially holy. The problem is to discover this normal method. The normal method must be the divine method. If we are partners with the Divine Being in all this ownership, it is necessary for us to know what his purposes are respecting the wealth which by his aid we have accumulated. And we know that he regards it all as material for character-building. The life is more than the meat; the soul is better than the house it lives in; the character is the supreme concern, to which all earthly possessions are subordinate and tributary. The question for every man is, then, How can I hold this property, and how can I use it so that the divine purpose can be realized in my conduct, and the divine life nourished in my soul? By what frugality, by what expenditure, by what investment, can I best realize God's will in my own life and in the lives of those about me? How can I administer this property in my hands so that it shall be a means of grace to me, and a benefit to my fellow-men? Any use of it that tends to enlarge my understanding, to refine and ennoble my tastes, to deepen my affections, to broaden my sympathies, to develop the essential humanity of my nature, will be a right use of it; for he who formed this nature of mine summons me to perfection, and has given me these good things to aid me in striving after perfection.

Any employment of my property which is calculated to promote the interests of character in my fellow-men must also be in accordance with the divine purpose. If it is my main purpose to hold and use my property in such a way that the coming of the kingdom of God may be hastened, and his will be done more perfectly in the world, then I am brought by my property into closer communion and dearer fellowship with him. When this purpose rules the life, labor is worship, and trade is a sacrament.

When we use property in this way we use it rightly, and so long as we use it rightly we have a right to use it. When we use it in any way which conflicts with the purpose for which God has given it to us, or which hinders the realization of that purpose, we are no longer in partnership with him, and our right is extinguished. You can have no moral right to any amount or any kind of property, the getting or the having of which makes you a worse man or keeps you from becoming a better man. Certainly, when we come down to the real rights in the case, we shall all admit that no man can acquire the moral right to become a knave. And if this is true, he can have no moral right to get or have that which makes him a bad man or hinders him from becoming a good man.

II. This doctrine that property is communion with God through the material world involves, as we have seen, certain obligations toward our fellow-men. The divine fatherhood implies the human brotherhood. If we hold what we have as members of one family, family affection must control the use of it. Our Father's will respecting our brethren, as well as ourselves, must be the law of our conduct. Not our own exclusive welfare, but the welfare of all the rest as well, we are bound to seek. We cannot be in communion with him while we are indifferent to the happiness of those who are dear to him. The doctrine that our property, be it much or little, must be made serviceable to the general welfare, as well as to our individual well-being, follows, therefore, from the principle which we have just been considering.

But we may easily establish the doctrine by a different course of reasoning. Let it be admitted as a principle of equity, *that one ought not to receive from any source great and constant benefits without making such return as he is able to make to his benefactors.* Now every human being, living in civilized society, and accumulating wealth through his relation to society, receives from society great and constant benefits; is aided by society most efficiently in this work of accumulating property; and ought, therefore, to hold and use his gains, not for his own exclusive benefit, but for the benefit, also, of his fellow-men.

We saw, in our study of the doctrine of property in land, that the land is a gift of God to the nation for the benefit of all the people. Let us suppose that the nation has found a way of dividing its patrimony equitably among the people, on such terms of use and ownership as are calculated to promote the welfare of all. Let us suppose that, as the result of this distribution, I have in my possession a piece of land. My title to it is perfectly equitable. I may cultivate it, or I may build on it a shop or a factory. By either of these methods, by agriculture or by mechanical industry, I may produce and accumulate property. Have I an exclusive right to the property I thus accumulate?

I cannot have any *exclusive* right to the land; this we have demonstrated. My right may be exclusive of the right of any other individual, but cannot be superior to the claims of the whole people. But may I not have an exclusive right to the products derived from the land by my own labor? This question is answered by all jurists in the affirmative. It is considered as fundamental to the doctrine of property, that every man should be protected in the enjoyment of the fruits of his labor; that his right to the wealth which he has created by his toil should be fully conceded. So far as jurisprudence can go, this principle is undoubtedly sound. Nor am I aware that ethics has any quarrel with law on this question. That value which a man by his own unaided toil has created may be his by exclusive right as long as he lives. Let us admit this. But the question comes back to every man, How much of the value of that property now in your hands was given to it by your own unaided toil?

Suppose you are a farmer; the wealth that you have gathered from the soil is not the fruit of your unaided labor. Nature has been helping you mightily, day by day and year by year. No small share of your wealth is due to the divine bounty of the soil. The Nation, acting as the representative of God, has permitted you to use this portion of its domain, and it expects you to use it for the public welfare. Some things you have no right to do with this land which you are cultivating: you have no right to impoverish it, so that it shall have less power to sustain life in coming time than it now possesses. *You are bound, therefore, to use part of the product of your labor on the land in keeping the land fertile.* This generation has no right to bequeath the land, stripped and despoiled of its life-giving power, to the generation following. The land is not put into your possession for any such purpose. So, then, it cannot be said that any man has an exclusive right to all that he can produce by his own labor upon the land, even though he may hold the land by the most equitable of all titles.

But, turning from the case of the cultivator of the soil, let us consider the much simpler case of the artisan. His standing-room on the soil he has gained by an equitable distribution; the materials on which he expends his labor he has obtained, let us suppose, by fair exchanges; the goods which he produces by his labor, or the money which he receives in exchange for them, are his property. Shall he say that property of this sort is exclusive? that nobody else has any claims upon it? He will not be able to maintain that position very long, for the tax-collector soon appears and demands a considerable slice of it. And if he protests that this property is all the fruit of his labor, the answer will be: "Be that as it may, you must contribute a part of the fruits of your labor for the maintenance of the government. While you have been working, the state has been standing near, warning off trespassers, guarding you against thieves, protecting you in the acquisition and enjoyment of your property. Your gains would have been much smaller and far less secure if the government had not been vigilant and strong to defend your rights. In fact, the government has been coöperating with you in this industry. It is not true that this property in your hands is the fruit of your unaided labor. The state, through its officers and magistrates, has been aiding you very powerfully in your work, by furnishing you protection. You owe to the state some return for this important service. Besides, every man who lives in a land like this must do something for the public welfare. Most likely he obtained the education which fits him to be an intelligent workman, in the public schools. Some contribution from the fruits of his labor is due to the state for the maintenance of these schools. And there are many other matters of general well-being, interests of intelligence and philanthropy for which the state must provide, and every citizen must bear his part.

It appears, therefore, that no man who lives in society has an exclusive right to the fruit of his own labor. Some part of that is due, by law and by equity, to the commonwealth.

But, passing by these civil relations and these legal claims, when these are satisfied, is there no further rightful claim upon the man's possessions? I am not asking about the demands of charity; I am speaking of the equities of the case, — of what is *due* from this man to others for value received. And I maintain that no man can accumulate property, in a social order like that in which we live, without incurring a heavy debt to society, — a debt that is by no means discharged when he has paid his taxes. Our fortunes, as well as our characters, are due in no small part to our environment. Those who have amassed property in this generation have done so by the use of a vast system of social and industrial machinery, which has been furnished to them without money and without price. They are the heirs of all the past ages of discovery, of invention, of study, of experiment, of organizing intelligence. Society has brought all these enormous gains down through the generations, and laid them at their feet. All these methods of communication, swift and cheap, by which time is multiplied and space is annihilated; all this wonderful utilization of natural force in machinery; all this mechanism of exchange, so intricate, and yet so beautiful in its action; all these systems of industrial organization, — what is all this but the costly and magnificent provision made by society for the use of the individual? It is only because this provision has been made that large gains are possible to honest men. In no past time could property be accumulated by honest industry and enterprise as rapidly as it can be to-day. There were rich Romans, but their gains were gotten by rapine or extortion. There are rich Americans, too, whose wealth is mainly plunder; but there are many others who by fairly legitimate means have acquired large possessions. This they never could have done had they not been the beneficiaries of a social and industrial order in which everything was made ready for their hands. To the society from which they have received so much they ought to make some adequate return. All such men, as Professor Graham has said, "owe something more than they can ever hope to pay, to science, to civilization, to mankind generally, but especially to the living generation of their own countrymen, as the present usufructuaries of the blessings of civilization. . . . These men, who have drawn so much, owe much; but only a rarely exceptional man acknowledges the debt, and by means of hospital, scientific college, or other bounty distributes again to his countrymen and civilization part of what through them he has gathered."[1] Such cases are not so exceptional on our side of the sea as they are on Professor Graham's side, but among us they are far less common than they ought to be. And the fact to be kept continually in sight is, that such use of his large gains for the public benefit is not charity on the rich man's part, but only a fair requital for services rendered him. Whoever holds property holds it subject to an equitable claim of this nature, a claim growing out of the conditions under which it was acquired. He may have gained it by legitimate industry or enterprise; nevertheless, the fruits of all legitimate industry or enter-

[1] *The Social Problem*, p. 457.

prise are, in these days, very largely a dividend upon an enormous accumulation of social capital, of which the successful man has had the use. This social capital is the sum of those "inappropriable utilities" of which Professor Clark has written so suggestively.[1] Many of the finest and most precious of the utilities created by human labor cannot be appropriated by individuals. They cannot be monopolized, they cannot be entailed or transmitted by bequest; they are the gains of civilization. Of these every man avails himself when he sets out to accumulate a fortune. And the obligation rests on him to see that this social capital is not wasted in his handling of it, — to transmit it to those who come after him in as good condition as he received it from those who went before him.

A very large part of this social capital consists of those subtle elements of confidence and good-will which give life to all our industrial and commercial operations. The organization of labor, the mechanism of exchange, are the product of these elements. The property that has been gained by the action of these forces ought to be administered so that these forces shall not be weakened. They who use their possessions ostentatiously, arrogantly, selfishly, in such a way as to express contempt for their less fortunate fellow-men, and to earn the distrust of their neighbors, are doing what they can to build up barriers between classes, and to prevent that harmonious social coöperation by

[1] *Philosophy of Wealth*, chap. xi.

which the accumulation of property is made possible. They are destroying the ladder by which they have ascended.

This social capital is the fruit, also, of the labors of a happy, hopeful, independent, energetic, enterprising people, — a people mentally alert and morally vigorous. No other kind of people could have made such gains. The whole population has shared in the production of this social wealth. It is in those lands where the people are free, and where the gates of opportunity are open to all, and only there, that these gains have been made. In our own land, especially, invention, discovery, enterprise, are in the air; faith in the future, hope of prosperity, love for the native land, have made us a happy and a prosperous people. Many of our keenest thinkers, our greatest inventors, our finest organizers, our bravest leaders, have come from the ranks of the toilers. A great share of these "inappropriable utilities" by which we have all been enriched has thus been contributed by those of lowly origin. Now, whatever lessens the intelligence, the hopefulness, the moral vigor of the masses of the people impairs the value of that social capital by the use of which the more prosperous among us make their gains. Whatever tends to make the working people sullen, spiritless, indifferent to the general welfare, tends to undermine the foundations on which our prosperity rests. Unless we can have a happy, hopeful, enterprising populace, the vast possibilities of honest acquisition and secure possession will quickly vanish away. And the men who have gained property by means of these wholesome and helpful social conditions have a great responsibility for their preservation. Especially are the men who employ labor bound to see that those whom they employ lose no jot of heart or hope in this relation. The man who gathers about him a hundred or a thousand workmen, and, after enriching himself by means of their labor, turns them out into society filled with hate and spite and suspicion, completely out of harmony with the age in which they live, is one of the worst of malefactors. No matter how successful he may have been in a material point of view, the wealth which he has produced with his machinery is a paltry contribution to society when compared with the social capital which he has destroyed in his unsocial relations with his workmen. Just as the farmers of this generation have no right to "skin" the land and pass it over to the next generation robbed of its life-giving powers, so the men who have enjoyed the mighty accumulation of social capital which consists so largely in the intelligence and morality and trustworthiness and good-will and hopefulness and happiness of the people, and who have made, by means of it, accumulation of property, larger or smaller, have no right to "skin" society of this social wealth, and leave the world poorer than they found it in these qualities. As the farming class is bound by the highest of all obligations to give back to the land enough of its product to preserve its productive energies unimpaired, so "the present usufructuaries of the blessings of civilization" are bound to make liberal return to society of the wealth that they have gathered, and to make this return in ways that shall tend to preserve those moral qualities in the people which are the source of all the productive energies of society. There are a great many ways in which this can be done. Property may be used to promote the intelligence, the virtue, and the happiness of the whole people by numberless beneficent ministrations. By the building of churches that shall not be private religious club-houses, but places of assembly and instruction for the public; by the founding of schools of science and art; by the establishment of libraries and museums and reading-rooms and coffee-houses and public baths and public gardens and foundations for free lectures, — by all these and many other such methods, wealth may be used to promote the public welfare and preserve the public morals, and to brighten and bless the life of the people. And when it is so used, remember well, it is not charity in any true sense of the word; it is simply the payment of an honest debt, — a payment which law cannot compel, but which the highest principles of equity most solemnly enjoin.

By one path we reached the truth that property is communion with God through the material world; by another path we have come to the complementary truth that property is fellowship with men through the material world. It is only through the love of God that we gain a just title to what we have; it is only in the love of our neighbors that it is rightly possessed and equitably used.

III. Property is power. If only those possessions which we have rightfully acquired are in the truest sense our property, it is nevertheless true that our possessions, however we may have gained them, confer upon us while we hold them a kind of power. Money is power. Wealth is power. In the use of this power a heavy responsibility rests on all those who hold it. It is not those alone who have much by whom this responsibility is incurred; they who have little bear it in their just proportion. It is not merely with his surplus, with what he holds after his desires are satisfied, that a man has power to do good or evil; there is power, also, to bring blessing or bale to many in that which he uses day by day.

I am not now speaking of the wealth which is counted as capital in the organization of business, in the employment of labor. That use of wealth involves more direct and obvious obligations, of which I shall speak farther on. I am dealing now with what we devote to our own enjoyment, with the power that we wield in the spending of money. We are all able to see that wealth employed in production imposes great responsibilities on those who employ it; but we do not so clearly see that in the consumption of wealth an equal obligation is incurred; that consumption as well as production is an exercise of power. In production most of us work under orders, and the responsibility rests on those who employ us; in consumption we exercise our powers directly, and if mischief is done the fault is ours alone.

Here is a mechanic on Saturday night with twelve dollars in his pocket, the wages of his week's work. It is not a large sum, but there is power in it, — power to do vast harm to him and to those dependent on him; power to confer great benefits upon him and upon them. Naturally our thoughts go first, as his thoughts should go, to the effect which will be produced by the expenditure of this money upon his life and the lives of those for whom he is responsible. It will bring to him and to them shelter, food, comfort, beauty, culture, — no great amount of these commodities and values, but enough, if judiciously used, to keep them in good health and hope till pay-day comes round again. There is power even in a few coppers or dimes to open for this man and his children some of the richest treasures of the human intellect; for the forty-eighth part of it he can buy the poems of Milton or of Scott, — more books than he can find leisure to read before the next Saturday night. And there are innocent pleasures, not a few, that he may easily command for himself and his household with a small fraction of his week's earnings. There is power here which will bring into his home health and wisdom and comfort and good cheer, if it be rightly used.

On the other hand, there are infinite energies of destruction and desolation in this small sum if it be wrongly used. It may be expended in debauching this workman's manhood; it may toll him into vile companionships and dens of infamy; it may purchase for him suffering and shame; it may fill his home with madness and terror and despair. A world of cursing as well as of blessing lives in this workman's weekly wage; and many there be who choose to buy with it, for themselves and for their wives and little ones, cursing instead of blessing.

But the money in this workman's pocket has power, not only over his own life and the life of his household, but over the lives of those in whose hands he will place it. This is the fact on which I desire to fix your attention. These twelve dollars constitute a demand for commodities or services of one sort or another. The money will be spent, and the spending of the money will set people at work in various places, on various objects. If the workman spends it week by week for beef and flour and sugar and tea and coal and house-rent and clothing and books and newspapers, his demand for these commodities sets people at work to furnish them. If he spends a good share of it in the saloon for beer or whiskey, he helps to create a demand for beer and whiskey, and for a multiplication of the places where beer and whiskey are sold; if he spends it in the gambling-places, he increases the demand for the services of gamblers and for the maintenance of the dens that they infest; if he spends it in any vicious or debasing indulgence, he becomes the employer of those who furnish this indulgence, and pays them for their service. The money in this workman's pocket, and the money in your pocket and mine as well, is power over the lives of other men. The manner in which we spend our money determines the manner in which some of our neighbors spend their time and strength. If we exchange it all for things useful and wholesome and beautiful, we employ them in producing such things. If we part with it for things harmful and worthless and debasing, we employ them in producing such things. If there are, as I estimate, every Saturday night, thirty thousand dollars in the pockets of the people of the city where I live, destined to be paid during the coming week for intoxicating liquors, that demand of thirty thousand dollars is very likely to put more than a thousand people in motion to distill and brew and distribute such beverages. This money, thus devoted, is the power that drives this drunkard-making machinery. I am aware that there is another side to this matter, — that the supply does something to create the demand; but the deeper and more important economical fact is that the supply is in much larger measure evoked by the demand.

"Whenever we spend money," says Mr. Ruskin, "we of course set people at work; *that is the meaning of spending money*. . . . Well, your shallow people, because they see that, however they spend money, they are always employing somebody, and therefore doing some good, think and say to themselves that it is all one how they spend it, — that all their apparently selfish luxury is in reality unselfish, and is doing just as much good as if they gave all their money away, or perhaps more good; and I have heard foolish people even declare it as a principle of political economy that whoever invented a new want conferred a good on the community. . . . Granted that whenever we spend money, for whatever purpose, we set people to work, and passing by, for the moment, the question whether the work we set them to is all equally healthy and good for them, we will assume that whenever we spend a guinea we provide an equal number of people with healthy maintenance for a given time. But, by the way in which we spend it, we entirely direct the labor of those people during that given time. We become their masters or mistresses, and we compel them to produce within a certain period a certain article. Now, that article may be a useful and lasting one, or it may be a useless and perishable one; it may be one useful to the whole community, or useful only to ourselves. And our selfishness and folly or our virtue and prudence are shown, not by our spending money, but by our spending it for the wrong or the right thing; and we are wise and kind, not in maintaining a certain number of people for a given period, but only in requiring them to produce during that period the kind of things which shall be useful to society, instead of those which are only useful to ourselves."[1] In these words of a master a thought is clearly stated which we have need to ponder. The power over the lives of other men which we always exercise when we spend money ought to be exercised with far more caution and conscientiousness than we are wont to use.

Spending money for vicious indulgences not only harms ourselves; it demoralizes those whom we thus employ to furnish us these vicious indulgences. The hundreds of millions of dollars that are annually consumed in this country for vice are simply devoted to employing hundreds of thousands of men and women as the purveyors and ministers of vice. Woe to those who use their power for such infernal purposes!

In expending our money for enjoyments that are not vicious, there is also need of care and conscientiousness. Many things are offered for sale into which the worker's life was wrought. Not a little of our modern manufacture is slow murder. We do not always know its products when they are offered to us; but when we do know them we shall spurn them. I think that we ought to take pains to detect them. It is the demand for cheap goods that is responsible, to a large extent, for starvation wages. The victims of the sweater are really the victims of the consumers.

So far as we may be able, we shall use the

[1] *Political Economy of Art*, p. 41.

power intrusted to us in the encouragement of healthful industries by which things useful and beautiful are produced, in industries in which the laborers gain a decent subsistence and increase the nation's store of all that is good and fair, and in the command of services which shall ennoble, and not degrade, those who render them.

Upon those who have large properties this doctrine presses solemnly. Much will be required of him to whom much is given. The possession of great power brings great responsibilities. The man who consumes his tens of thousands yearly, does he comprehend the power that he wields, and the obligation to use it beneficently? Not unconscious is he of his power. The supple hinges of the knee crooked before him every day keep him well advised of that. The effect of this power on the lives of those about him who want a share of his money is evident enough to him. He knows that there is a subtle energy in this wealth which he possesses that will warp the conscience of some men and corrupt the virtue of some women; that there are many round about him, whom he could not convince by reason nor persuade by affection, whom he can bend to his purposes by the use of this power. This money of his will purchase commercial falsehoods and frauds, newspaper adulation, votes, nominations, legislative acts, judicial decisions; what cannot money do, if it is shrewdly manipulated? Unhappily for this land, there are vast numbers of men among us who possess this power, and who are not slow to employ it for such unrighteous purposes.

Others there are who possess the same power, and who seek to use it wisely and helpfully for the succor of the weak, for the support of the heavy laden, for the defense of public virtue and the enlargement of public welfare. In the service of these great interests money is not omnipotent; there is much that it cannot do; there are ends which it cannot compass; there are ministries for which a loftier and a mightier power is needed than that which is incarnated in the substances and the symbols of material wealth. But there is much that it can do; it is a force by which, when it is rightly directed, vast and beneficent effects may be wrought; and it will be a good day for the church of God and the world of men when the nature of this power is better understood, and when it is turned to consecrated uses; when property is seen by all who call themselves Christians to be rightly held only through communion with God, and rightly used only for the welfare of men.

V.

THE LABOR QUESTION.

It is sometimes denied that there is any labor question, or, at any rate, that there is just foundation for one. A few crazy anarchists, it is said, are trying to stir up discontent among the working people; but the people at large are not really discontented, nor have they any reason to be. They were never so well off as they are to-day; they would not think of complaining, if these imported agitators, and a few doctrinaire philanthropists who might be in a better business, did not keep putting mischievous notions into their heads. Chicago happily hanged her anarchists; if every other city will select a few of its most conspicuous labor reformers and send them to Terra del Fuego, we shall get along very well.

This kind of talk is common in some quarters, albeit the tone of such objurgations is a little less acrimonious than it was a few years ago. The struggles between employers and employed, which are becoming more and more frequent and general; the combinations of workmen, which are certainly growing formidable; and such an exhibition of political strength as has been furnished in some of our elections, make it plain that discontent exists, far deeper and more pervasive than any little band of fanatical agitators could have fomented. During the last summer, in three States and in one Territory, troops were called out to suppress insurrections of laborers. A labor question there certainly is, and it is the most urgent question before this country at this hour. To say that there is no ground for this uprising is to say that the great mass of the working people are either so ignorant that they cannot understand their own circumstances and their own needs, or so unreasonable and selfish that they are willing to destroy the industries of the country for the sake of gratifying their whims and jealousies. I am not willing to bring such an accusation against them. Doubtless they sometimes exaggerate the evils of their condition, and there is often want of true perspective in the view which they take of social questions; one-sided and distorted representations are even found in the books and newspapers which speak in the interests of capital. But no such general restlessness and dissatisfaction ever spring up in society without an adequate cause; and the idea of holding a few leaders responsible for all this fever and tumult is like holding the pimples on the skin responsible for the poison in the blood, or the flying chimney-pots for the force of the gale. Those persons who belittle the present agitation after this manner exhibit profound ignorance of the real conditions of society.

But is not this disturbance, after all, destitute of justification? many are inquiring. Are not the working classes better off to-day than they ever were before? I wish it were possible to give a precise and conclusive answer to this question. I can quote to you strong authorities on both sides; but the question is so large that it is almost impossible to speak about it with any sense of comprehensiveness and assurance. That the average wage-worker of to-day can buy with his *daily* wage more food and clothing and fuel than the average wage-worker of a century or two ago could buy with his daily wage is undoubtedly true. But the question is one of annual rather than of daily wages, and the wage-worker of to-day loses so much time through failures, depressions, changes of business due to changing fashions, and to the oppressive discriminations of the railroads, that it is an open question whether his earnings *year by year* are larger, counted in necessaries of life, than those of the wage-worker of former times. We are often pointed to the improved manner of living of the workingmen of to-day, to the variety and fineness of their food, to the many articles of comparative luxury that are found in their homes. It is true that the standard of comfort, as thus exhibited, is higher than once it was; but the standard of comfort is almost always fixed — unwisely, of course — in the days of prosperity. If a man receives a dollar and a half a day when he is at work, he generally adjusts his expenditure to an income of a dollar and a half a day; when the work ceases, if he does not appeal to the city or the Benevolent Society for aid, he runs in debt at the grocery and the butcher shop and the coal dealer's, and his rent falls in arrears. When work begins again there is a debt to pay. It is hard to reduce the scale of living, to purchase plainer food and clothing than that to which he has been accustomed, and the debt lingers and accumulates, and is often at length dishonored. This is bad economy and bad morality; but it is the natural result of an industrial condition as feverish and shifting as ours is at the present time. The fact that a high standard of comfort appears to have been set up in many workingmen's homes is not, then, a sure indication of real prosperity. Many of them cannot afford to live at the rate at which we find them living; if they should make their *daily* expenditure conform to their *annual* income, they would live far more plainly than they do.

The census of 1880 reports 253,840 manufacturing establishments in the United States, employing 2,738,930 hands, and paying $947,919,674 in wages. This is an average annual wage of $309 a year. These "hands" include a good many women and children. The estimate of Mr. Carroll D. Wright, based upon that census and other investigations, was that the workingman of ten years ago earned on an average about $400 a year; that, he thought, might be regarded as the sum on which the average workingman's family must subsist. President Harrison's last message gives the figures of the census of 1890 for the mechanical industries of seventy-five leading cities; by these figures it appears that the average annual wage in these cities has increased from $386 in 1880 to $547 in 1890, or more than forty-one per cent. I think that no one will be more surprised at this intelligence than the wage-workers themselves. If so great an improvement in their condition has taken place within the last ten years, it is a little strange that they should not have heard of it. It would appear that the tabulators of the census bureau must have got hold of facts which are known to nobody else in the community. How these averages were made up we do not know. There is no greater snare to the average investigator than the doctrine of averages. The pitfall is one into which a good many of us, at one time or another, have fallen. It will never do to add the average wage of seventy-five different cities together and divide that sum by seventy-five in order to get the average wage of the whole laboring population of those cities. Suppose that Waltham, for example, has 2,000 highly skilled workers whose average wage is $600, and that New York has 100,000 workers whose average wage is $300. The rash statistician might say that the average wage of workers in those two cities was $450. In fact, it would be $305.98.

There is, also, much room for sophistication in the classification of hands. If the superintendents, managers, overseers, and clerks are under one computation reckoned out, and under another reckoned in, your statistical comparisons are worthless. There is reason for believing that statistics are often collected for political purposes; in such cases their conclusions are to be distrusted. It is an infinite pity that this whole business cannot be wholly dissociated from politics, and placed in the hands of a permanent bureau of competent investigators.

I am not, therefore, inclined to believe that there has been in these seventy-five cities an increase in wages of forty-one per cent. within the last ten years; nor is it probable that the average annual wage of laborers in these cities amounts to $547. We must wait for a much more careful examination of these reports before we accept this optimistic estimate. If it turns out that the average workingman's family has had even twenty-five per cent. added to its income within the last ten years, I shall be greatly surprised. But let us suppose that this is true. Let us concede, for the sake of the argument, that their income now amounts to $500.

Certainly life can be supported upon this income, if it is carefully used; but it is a narrow and meagre subsistence that it will furnish to a family of five. Rent, in most cases, will absorb one fifth of it; that leaves eighty dollars a year, one dollar and fifty-three cents a week for each one, to pay for food, clothing, fuel, lights, medicine, amusement, travel, and incidental expenses. A family can live on this; many families do; but not, surely, in princely fashion. Sit down and cipher out the possible bill of fare, the allowance for wardrobe, the minimum of coal and oil required, the remainder for luxuries and pleasures, and you can easily convince yourself that it is not a sin to be dissatisfied with an annual income of five hundred dollars.

This penury would be endured, no doubt, much more cheerfully if there were not so many signs of plenty on every side. The same high authority which puts the wage-worker's income of ten years ago at four hundred dollars a year estimated that those living on salaries would receive, on an average, one thousand dollars a year. To some of us this would not seem excessive; but the difference between five hundred dollars a year and one thousand dollars a year, to a family of five, is the difference between penury and abundance. The smaller sum barely suffices for the commonest and coarsest needs; the larger sum brings into the house light and cheer, beauty and enjoyment. The value of the alleviations and the comforts which this extra five hundred dollars signifies can be very imperfectly estimated save by those who once enjoyed them, and are now forced to dispense with them.

If the people who live on salaries have, as a rule, so much more to spend than the people who work for wages, it is certain that the owners of the capital and the captains of industry are still more prosperous. We have no means of guessing what the average income of persons of this class may be. Some of them make but small gains and live in a simple manner; but the palaces and the carriages and the silks and the furs and the diamonds and the jewelry that we all see are proof enough that some of them have contrived to command the spending of a good many thousands a year.

It is this contrast of the luxury and splendor round about him with his own scanty fare and sharp limitations that causes, as we have already seen, the laborer's discontent. "The laboring classes," says Professor Graham, "do all the monotonous and disagreeable and dangerous work for our benefit, for the benefit of the classes above them. They have little or no real liberty, which is incompatible with their hard work, and they have little money over their own needs and those of their families. . . . On the other hand, life for the fortunate was never, in any age nor under any civilization, a greater gift, or susceptible of grander possibilities than it is to-day. Even for men with only moderate incomes life was never more enjoyable, never promised so much. And the toiling multitude see not only much of this to arouse their envy, but they see on all sides all the outward and splendid and ostentatious signs of limitless wealth. . . . It is comparative poverty in the midst of this boundless and ever-increasing wealth; it is comparative slavery of the toilers in the midst of increased liberty, leisure, luxury, and the increased pleasure and power which wealth in our time confers, that makes the grievance of the laborer and raises the grudge in his heart." [1]

"In perfectly simple states of society," says Hermann Lotze, "the various dispositions which even there have place appear side by side, as if they all had an equal right to exist, just as the different kinds of animals, for none of which is it any reproach to be what it is: it is to a high degree of refinement that there is first opposed as its antitype that coarseness which, while it knows all the newly discovered and newly developed moral relations, despises or misuses all of them. Just in the same way, poorness of external appearance is no reproach, is often picturesque, at a stage of civilization in which men have few wants, and satisfy these in the most primitive and simple manner. On the other hand, this same poverty assumes the peculiar character of squalor, when it appears in the midst of a society the life of which is based upon a very complicated and intricately branching system of satisfying human wants. Poverty, taking isolated and disconnected fragments from this system, becomes subject to wants which it has no assured permanent and adequate means of satisfying." [2]

One may be naked and unashamed in Paradise; but when the fashion of wearing clothes becomes universal, nakedness becomes embarrassing. Our miseries are mostly relative; and it is by compari-

[1] *The Social Problem*, pp. 5, 6.
[2] *Microcosms*, ii. 387.

son that the laborer has come to feel that he is not so well off as he ought to be, in the midst of the abundance which his labor has helped to create.

I am not disposed, however, to go very extensively into the discussion of the question whether the laborer is right or wrong in his opinion that he is losing ground, because the facts on which a safe judgment can be based are not accessible. It is largely a matter of impressions. But I confess that I am strongly inclined to take the workingman's view. My experience as a pastor for thirty years, of churches in manufacturing communities, and my close observation of the conditions of life among the working classes, do not lead me to believe that the problem of existence is growing easier for these people. Two or three tremendous facts confront me whenever I endeavor to put an optimistic construction upon present tendencies in the labor market. It is only a few years ago that we had, according to the careful estimates of Colonel Wright, one million laborers standing idle in the market-place because no man would hire them. These were not tramps; they were men who wanted to work, and could find nothing to do. This million of laborers represented, probably, three and a half or four million sufferers. For a whole year they waited for the paralyzed industries to revive. Can any one estimate the distress, the physical deterioration, the loss of moral stamina and self-respect, entailed by such a calamity? That is one fact. Another is, that these periods of industrial depression tend to return at shorter intervals, and to remain longer when they come. They are less violent than once they were, but more persistent. The dumb ague has succeeded to the chills and fever, in our industrial system. Every one of these industrial depressions pushes a multitude of families into the abyss of pauperism. The number of paupers seems to be diminishing in Great Britain; it is as surely increasing in this country, if we count among the paupers all those who receive outdoor relief in our cities during the winters. The proportion of the population of the cities that is aided from the public purse or from private charity is becoming ominously large. The alarming growth of this element in our population has led to the formation, everywhere, of charity organization societies, whose twofold function is the relief of the needy and the repression of pauperism. In the presence of these facts, I am not able to take so hopeful a view as some wise men take of the present condition of our working people. It seems to me that an army out of whose ranks such a host of stragglers and invalids and cripples is constantly dropping cannot be in a very vigorous condition, physically or morally. And without trying to analyze the figures of the statisticians, which are too incomplete to be of any great value, I come back to the fact that the working people generally think they have a grievance, and are up in arms to redress it. The rapid growth of the trades-unions and the Knights of Labor, the spread of the new labor party, and many other such tokens indicate the workingman's view of the case. The politicians are beginning to listen with great respect to his complaints; some of the soundest of our political economists go part of the way with him in his demands, and not a few clear-headed business men are ready to assent to the words of Chauncey M. Depew, president of the New York Central Railroad, and one of the largest employers of labor in this country: "The workingman has a grievance. We may not clearly understand it; he may not know very well what it is; but it exists." Is it possible to find out what it is?

In the minds of some of the laborers, this grievance consists of the fact that the workman fails to receive the entire product of his labor. This, they insist, is the only equitable arrangement. "All wealth," they say, "is produced by labor; the men who produce it are entitled to the whole of it. They do not receive the whole of it; they receive, in fact, but a small share of it. The men who call themselves capitalists, or employers, get the most of it. This is the fundamental injustice. The whole organization of industry is on an iniquitous basis, and always has been. Under slavery, the capitalist employer took the whole of the workman's earnings, and gave him, so long as he found it profitable to do so, enough food and shelter to sustain his life. Under feudalism, the capitalist employer permitted the serf to work for himself certain days in the week, and required him to work for him the rest of the time. Under the wage system, the capitalist employer pays the workman a certain wage, but this wage is only a part of what the workman produces by his labor; the workman's labor creates a large surplus value which the capitalist employer takes for himself. He is not entitled to it. It all belongs to the man who produced it."

This is the substance of the doctrine of Karl Marx in his famous book on "Capital," which, through translations and expositions in newspaper articles and speeches in workingmen's assemblies, has filtered down into the minds of the people, and is greatly influencing the thought of the workmen on both continents at the present time. "Why do you talk of profit sharing?" said a workingman, rather indignantly, to me, not long ago, at the close of an address. "Why should the man who does the work *share* the wealth that he produces with anybody? Who else has any right to it but the man who produces it?" The extent to which this doctrine of Marx has permeated the thought of the wage-workers is not probably suspected by most of those who employ them. The manifestoes of the various labor organizations express this idea more or less clearly. The Knights of Labor speak moderately; they declare in their constitution that it is one of their aims "to secure for the workers the full enjoyment of the wealth they create."[1] The National Labor Union, in its Platform of Principles, affirms: "We further hold

[1] Art. II.

that all property or wealth is the product of physical or intellectual labor employed in productive industry, and in the distribution of the productions of labor. That laborers ought of right, and would, under a just monetary system, receive or retain the larger proportion of their productions,"[1] etc. The International Working People's Association thus expounds: "Our present society is founded on the expoliation of the propertiless classes by the propertied. The expoliation is such that the propertied (capitalists) buy the working force, body and soul, of the propertiless, for the price of the mere costs of existence (wages) and take for themselves, that is, steal, the amount of new values (products) which exceeds this price, whereby wages are made to represent the necessities instead of the earnings of the wage laborer."[2] The Socialistic Labor Party lays down this as the first plank of its platform: "Labor being the only creator of all wealth and civilization, it rightfully follows that those who perform all labor and create all wealth should enjoy the result of their toil."[3] Such ideas are current among our working people. Laveleye says that these doctrines of Marx, "translated into common language in petty socialist journals, have become the workingman's catechism throughout Germany,"[4] and the state-

[1] Quoted by Professor Ely in *The Labor Movement in America*, p. 335.

[2] *Ibid.* p. 359.

[3] *Ibid.* p. 366.

[4] *The Socialism of To-Day*, p. 24.

ment is not far from the truth with respect to our own country. What is more significant is the fact that these doctrines of Marx are drawn directly, by natural if not always quite fair deductions, from the teachings of orthodox political economy, from the propositions of Adam Smith and Ricardo and Bastiat. In the very first sentence of his famous book Adam Smith says, "The annual labor of every nation is the fund which originally supplies it with all the necessaries and conveniences of life which it annually consumes;"[1] and again, more expressly, "Labor alone, therefore, never varying in its own value, is alone the real standard by which the value of all commodities can at all times and places be estimated and composed."[2] Ricardo's theory of value rests also on this foundation. "All things become more or less valuable," he says, "in proportion as more or less labor was bestowed on their production."[3] Grant these premises, and the conclusions of Marx are inevitable. Here is a fine illustration of the speciousness of a purely deductive method in political economy. I do not think that the complaints and demands of the working people of to-day are wholly unreasonable, but they are partly so; and the element of unreason that they contain is a logical inference from the teachings of our most illustrious political economists. It is true that Smith and Ricardo somewhat modify their statements on this

[1] *Wealth of Nations*, p. 1. [2] *Ibid.* p. 34.
[3] *Political Economy*, ch. i. 1.

point; they are not always consistent with themselves; they saw, now and then, the complementary truth; but the emphasis of their teaching rests on these sentences which the Socialists have turned to good account.

The very first thing to do, in the conduct of this discussion, is, therefore, to get these erroneous ideas out of the minds of the working people. It is not true that labor is the sole cause of value or of wealth. Many substances and possessions have great value on which no labor has ever been expended. There are building-lots in every large city on which not a stroke of labor was ever performed, which possess great value. There are steep and barren hillsides all over this country on which no labor has ever been expended, but which will sell to-day for enormous sums of money, because it is known that beneath their rugged surfaces lie treasures of oil or coal or iron or marble. There are millions of acres of virgin soil in the West, never yet tickled with the hoe or embroidered with the plowshare, which are of great value to their fortunate possessors. If labor is the sole source of value, then all differences in the value of commodities must be due to differences in the amount of labor bestowed upon them. But land on the principal street of my own city is probably worth fifteen hundred dollars a front foot, whereas land on the outskirts of the city is worth, perhaps, ten dollars a front foot; and far more labor has been bestowed on the cheaper land than on the dearer. Mr. Macleod has some trenchant talk along this line which I may as well quote:—

"If labor be the sole cause of value, a thing once produced by labor must always have value, and the same value; but this is notoriously contrary to experience, because it is notorious that a thing may have value in one place, and not in another. . . . Take a bag of sovereigns among the Eskimos, and where would their value be? . . . If any one were to set up a manufactory of watches, or reclaim land and grow fine fields of wheat, in the centre of Australia, where there was no demand for the watches or the corn, where would their value be? Moreover, if labor be the sole cause of value, if a thing is once produced, its value could never vary: which is Ricardo's express doctrine. But this is contrary to all experience, because things, after they have been produced, and all labor upon them has been ended, constantly vary in their value from day to day, and from hour to hour, and from year to year. Thus, pictures by one master constantly rise in value, and pictures by another master diminish in value, long after the hands that painted them are cold in the grave. . . . In the reign of George III., there was a very widespread fashion to wear shoe-buckles; this manufacture employed a very large number of persons. All of a sudden these buckles went out of fashion; the demand totally ceased; and the people employed in making them were thrown into the greatest distress. But, according to Ricardo, the labor of the men who made the buckles was of the same value when there was a demand for them and when there was no demand for them. Some years ago, the fashion of ladies wearing straw bonnets suddenly went out, and the manufacturers of them . . . were thrown into great distress. But, according to Ricardo, their labor was of exactly the same value when there was a demand for straw bonnets and when there was none. Hence we see that even with respect to material things there are many upon which no labor was ever bestowed which have great value and different degrees of value; and even of those upon which labor has been bestowed, the labor is not the force or cause of their value."[1]

There is also a large class of values of which this is even more evidently true. General Tom Thumb was the possessor of a commodity which had great economical value, and by means of which he realized large revenues. His diminutiveness in stature was a marketable commodity. It possessed the property of gratifying a human desire, — not the noblest of human desires, indeed, nor the meanest, either, — curiosity. But this diminutiveness of stature which was the source of wealth to General Thumb was not the product of labor.

The manager of the American Opera hears a phenomenal voice ringing through the corridor of the hotel where he is sojourning. Immediately he

[1] *Elements of Economics*, i. 246.

seeks out the chambermaid who is the possessor of the voice, and offers her maintenance and wages if she will render him service under the direction and training of his chief musicians. There was money in that voice, as the saying is. But the value thus discovered was not the result of labor.

Here are two young men, equal in ability, in experience, in training, working side by side in the same office. There is a certain position of responsibility to be filled by those who have watched them carefully and know them both, and one of them is taken, and the other left. Why? They are equally industrious, equally intelligent, equally competent. So far as their abilities could be improved by labor, they are equally qualified. But one of them is more trustworthy than the other. His superior trustworthiness has a distinct economic value. It is worth money in the market. He who possesses it can command a larger income than he who possesses it not. But this is a purely moral quality; it is not, in any sense of the word, the product of labor. Neither the quality itself, nor the gain by which it is remunerated, can be said to be the fruit of labor.

It is very clear, then, that wealth is not wholly the product of labor. Labor is one of the sources of wealth, but it is by no means the only source. A great many other forces besides the labor force enter as factors into the product which we call the wealth of the nation. And when the manual laborers claim the whole product as theirs by right of creation, they make an extravagant claim, for which sound reason furnishes no justification.

Every product of human labor possesses value in proportion as it satisfies some human desire. If the maker produces it for himself, he may be supposed to know what his own desire is, and how to satisfy it. But if he makes it with a view to exchanging it for money or other products of labor, then its exchangeability will depend on the intelligence, the skill, and the taste with which it is made. It is not simply the amount of muscular exertion expended in making it that determines its value; it is its fitness to satisfy the desires of those to whom he will offer it in exchange. A workman with great intelligence, skill, and taste will produce articles that will gratify the desires of many, and he will have no difficulty in exchanging them on very favorable terms for money, or for the products of other workers. A workman with little intelligence, skill, and taste will produce articles that nobody will want, and will find it hard to exchange his products on any terms for those of other workers. It is plain, then, that it is intelligence, skill, and taste that give value to the products of labor, more than the merely mechanical or muscular force by which they are produced.

Let us suppose that one workman who possesses these intellectual qualities in an unusual degree finds another who lacks them, and enters into an arrangement with him. "You work hard enough," he says to his neighbor, "and you are not a bad workman, but you do not seem to get on. You are always busy, but either you do not make the right kind of things, or else you do not make them at the right time or in the right way, and nobody seems to want what you produce. Let me guide you. I will furnish you plans and patterns ; I will show you what to make and how to make it ; work under my direction, and I will guarantee a product that will exchange for twice as much as you got for yours last year." The bargain is made, and the promise is fulfilled ; the inefficient workman's product is thus doubled. Is he justified, now, in claiming the whole of this product ? Can he truthfully say that his labor is the cause of it all ? Is it not true that the intelligence, the skill, and the taste of the other workman have produced half of it ? And if the superior workman should take a part of this increased product for himself, and should leave the rest of it for the inferior workman, thus largely increasing the inferior workman's income, would there be any injustice in the operation ? Would not the inferior workman have reason for gratitude rather than complaint ?

Now, it is the sober fact, and no intelligent workingman will deny it, that a very large number of those who labor with their hands lack the intelligence necessary for the best employment of their own powers ; and the product of their labor is greatly increased when they put themselves under the direction of some person of superior taste and judgment, and let him direct their industry. When they so labor the product is not wholly the fruit of their labor, it is largely the fruit of the intelligence by which their labor has been directed; and a part of it ought to be conceded as the just recompense of this directing intelligence. The working-man who does not frankly make this concession shows that there is something wrong either with his head or with his heart.

There is still another aspect of the case of which it is necessary to speak. Let us suppose that, in the old days of the domestic system of manufacture, two weavers dwelt in adjoining cottages, plying their avocation. One of them, who was a good workman, spent in the market or at the alehouse every cent of his earnings, and devoted his leisure time to idleness or diversion. The other, who was equally skillful, saved a portion of his wages every week, and spent his leisure in study. By and by the active mind of this sober workman begins to exercise itself upon the problem of an improved loom, and in due season he has wrought it out; in his evenings and his holidays he has built it; and it proves, on trial, to have three times the speed of the old loom. Then he goes to his neighbor with this proposition: "Put aside your old loom, and take my new one and weave for me. I have saved money enough to live on for a year, while I build more looms." How much, now, should the hired weaver receive for his work? He can weave with this improved loom three times as much cloth as he wove the year before. The earnings of this man with this machine are trebled. Is he entitled to the whole of this? Has not the man who invented and built the loom a just claim upon a part of it? The ingenuity that produced this machinery, and the frugality that enabled the owner to live without wages while the other man was using it, are not these entitled to some reward? Suppose that the owner of the loom should give to the other half of what he was able to earn with the improved machine; would the other have any reason for complaint? His income would have been increased fifty per cent. by his new employer. For that increase, it seems to me, thanks, and not curses, would be due.

Now, this ingenious workman, with his improved machine and his little hoard saved to live upon while he makes a new loom, is a capitalist employer. The loom and the little hoard are his capital. By means of this capital he employs his neighbor. The money earned is the joint production of the capital of the one and the labor of the other. This capital assists very efficiently in the work of production. It is entitled, I think, to a share of the product. And whenever any man, by legitimate industry and frugality and ingenuity and business capacity, is able to collect machinery and materials, and to organize the industry of his neighbors in such a way that the product of their labor is greatly increased, I am unable to see why he is not fairly entitled to a portion of the increased value thus produced. The theory that the workman has a right to the whole of it is irrational. It is only by accumulations of capital that labor can be organized and made efficient. The frugality that saves the capital is an indispensable condition of the organization of labor. To a part of the increased product resulting from the organization of labor the frugality that saves the capital is justly entitled.

I trust I have made it plain, even to the wayfaring man, that the maxims of Smith and Ricardo are untrue, and that the conclusions derived from them by Karl Marx and the Socialists are unsound. Labor is not the sole cause of wealth, nor is it the only measure of value. That which gives value to objects is the desire of men to possess them. The value thus set upon them leads men to work to produce them. Men do not value things simply because they have worked to produce them; they work to produce them because they value them. The labor of men of inferior intelligence is made more productive when it is directed by men of superior intelligence, and part of the increased product belongs of right to the intelligence that caused it. The productive power of labor is also vastly increased by organization and by the use of machinery; and part of this gain is due to those who have saved the capital, without which this organization could not be effected.

So far, therefore, as the workingmen of this country have come to entertain the monstrous notion that their labor is the sole cause of the wealth of this country, and that they are defrauded of their rights if they do not possess the whole of it, they are under a most lamentable and dangerous delusion, and the sooner they get it out of their heads the better for them and for the whole country. They do not all entertain this notion. A great many of them are quite too sensible to give place to such vagaries, even though the great names of Smith and Ricardo be summoned to give them currency. But these more reasonable workingmen, as I have said, are by no means satisfied with the existing state of things. "We are not," say they, "entitled to all the wealth produced; that is an extravagant idea. We know that the men who organize and manage the productive industries of the country are entitled to a liberal share of the wealth that they help to produce. But we think that the share which they are getting is too large. That is our grievance."

With this feeling I have already said that I sympathize. I doubt whether the wage-worker is getting his just proportion of the wealth he is helping to produce. In his efforts to improve his circumstances all men of good-will are his allies. It is essential to the welfare of the nation that the wage-workers receive their full share of the growing wealth. They must go forward at an equal pace with all the rest of their fellow-citizens; there must be no room in their minds for a just suspicion that they are being left behind.

Nevertheless, it is well to understand that the

natural limit to the improvement of their circumstances is never very distant. No such radical change in their lot as some of them are looking for is possible. It often seems to be imagined by laborers who are, and who have a right to be, discontented with their condition, that if a more perfect equalization of the national income could be effected, the share of laborers might be very greatly increased. But the fact is that such an equalization would do far less for the working classes than they generally suppose. Many computations have been made; I will not repeat them, because there is some question as to their accuracy; but the largest estimate of the national income which I have seen would give, if it were distributed with absolute equality, only about fifty-seven cents a day to each person. The family of four would get two dollars and twenty cents a day. And this is certain, — that to add twenty-five cents a day to the portion of each one would require an addition of $5,475,000,000 to the annual product of the nation. It must be evident to all, therefore, that the dreams of boundless luxury for everybody in which some workingmen are in the habit of indulging are not going to come true under any dispensation. And it is high time that a good many of them were thinking less about a great increase of wages, which in most cases is simply impossible, and more about making a wiser and more economical use of the wages they now receive, which in many cases is altogether possible.

Another fact is also worth bearing in mind by wage-workers. The manufacturing industries of the country are now carried on under a system in which large numbers of workmen are grouped under one management. Under this system there is great gain of economy and efficiency; the subdivision of labor, the multiplication of machinery, greatly cheapen production. Under this system, also, the employer may give the workman the greater part of his earnings, and still make large gains himself.

Here is a manufacturer who employs one thousand men. Let us suppose that the average net product of the labor of these men, after deducting the cost of raw materials and the expense of necessary repairs, is one dollar and sixty cents a day. The manufacturer pays his men an average wage of one dollar and fifty cents a day. By the aid of his capital he makes ten cents a day out of each man's labor. That is the portion of the product that he takes as the wages of management and remuneration for the use of his capital. Probably a good many of the men are the gainers by this arrangement; they would not be able, if they were working on their own hook, to earn so much as he gives them. Yet his profit on the labor of one thousand men, at ten cents a day for each, is more than thirty thousand dollars a year. The arrangement is beneficial to the men, and it is highly profitable to the employer. I know not how such combinations as these can be prevented under a wage system of industry, nor do I see that it is desirable to prevent them. The man who has the organizing ability to bring a thousand workmen together and keep them steadily employed, cheaply and skillfully to procure the material for their labor, and successfully to dispose of the product of their labor, is entitled to a large reward for this difficult service. Such abilities will always command a high remuneration. And when such abilities are exerted, as they often are, with a conscientious purpose to confer benefit on those employed, the relation between employer and workmen may be not only amicable, but fraternal.

Unhappily, this conscientious purpose is not always manifest. The capitalist employer may be a philanthropist; he is too apt to be a man with whom "business is business," and labor simply a commodity, with which his only concern is to buy it in the cheapest market, and sell its product in the dearest. Under the management of such employers, the large system of industry becomes a terrific engine of oppression. The division of labor, the multiplication of machinery, strip the individual workman of skill and versatility, and make the man the slave of the machine. Cutthroat competition among employers forces wages down to starvation figures, and then combination comes in to hold them down. Then the workmen begin to combine, and there is war. The employing class and the wage-workers array themselves against each other as natural enemies; in their bitter conflicts, production is crippled, trade is paralyzed, and the peace and security of society are sorely disturbed. Thus we have come to the condition now confronting us,—the break-down of the competition system.

It is, for many reasons, superfluous to consider what the fate of the working classes would be under a system of pure competition. Such a system we never had. The severities of its operation have always been tempered by justice and compassion. Some employers have always refused to take advantage of their working people and crowd down wages when the market was falling. But, for better or worse, that old competitive régime has lost its supremacy as the regulator of wages. Combination on both sides has, to a great extent, supplanted competition; and while the armies confront each other, the world awaits with doubt and fear the issue of the combat. The end of it all will be, no doubt, some important modifications of the industrial system.

But while the old order is changing to the new, it is of the utmost importance that these truths which we have been considering be kept before the people. That labor is not the sole cause of wealth; that the most efficient production of wealth requires an intelligent and skillful organization and direction of labor; that this intelligence and skill are causes of the production of wealth as truly as muscular power or manual dexterity; that the men who possess this organizing and directing ability will always command a large reward for their services; and that the improvement in the laborer's condition must be gradual, — these truths must not be forgotten. It will be salutary for the employing class to remember, also, that the cause which has brought them into their present straits, and has filled their future with apprehension, is the failure to mix with the competitive principle the proper moral correctives. Some measure of good-will has always been infused into these relations of employer and employed, but not enough. A fierce egoism has dragged the industrial world to the brink of chaos. The old competitive régime might have continued to exist indefinitely, if there had only been a general willingness to temper the severities of the economic law by the gentler motives of good-will. It is because men supposed that loving ourselves was the law of business, and that loving our neighbors was only for Sundays and missionary contributions and charitable associations, that all this tempest has arisen, and the foundations of the industrial deep have been broken up. The want of a Christian temper has brought us into this trouble; and the cultivation of a Christian temper is the one thing needful to bring us out of it. It will be necessary, now, to make some change of methods, in order that a somewhat more equitable distribution of the product of industry may be secured; but the best methods will be of little avail unless there is a better spirit on the part of both employers and workmen. The important lesson for workmen and employers to learn is that they are very near neighbors. Having learned this lesson, they may well remember that there is one law which will bring order out of this chaos. It is not Ricardo's law of wages, nor Malthus's law of population, nor Marx's law of surplus value; it is the simple, old-fashioned law, "Thou shalt love thy neighbor as thyself."

VI.

THE COLLAPSE OF COMPETITION.

THE Paradise predicted by the old economists as the result of the supreme and exclusive devotion of every man to his own interest seems to have been late in arriving; suspicions are now entertained in some quarters that it is a veritable Utopia. Those who believe that Christ's law is the perfect law of society are not surprised that an industrial order resting on an explicit denial of Christ's law should turn out to be industrial disorder, — Pandemonium rather than Paradise.

The regulative force of the system which is passing is, or rather was, competition. As expounded by the early economists, this competitive system possessed a great deal of theoretical beauty; it was delightful to contemplate the peace and prosperity which it would surely evolve, if it were only let alone. But the competition of which all these blessed results were predicated is perfect competition; that is to say, a competition in which all the competitors are perfectly free and perfectly equal. In a society where each man clearly understood his own interest, and had the power to pursue it without let or hindrance, the economic results of competition might be beneficent. But in a society where there are vast differences in physical and in mental equipment, where the strong and the weak, the wise and the ignorant, the fierce and the timid, are all commingled, it is idle to talk of perfect competition. In its best estate, Professor Clark tells us, competition resembles a race; in its worst estate it is more like a battle. Now, though it may be true that the race is not *always* to the swift nor the battle to the strong, that accidental or providential interferences may sometimes obstruct natural forces, these are exceptions to the general rule; in the great majority of cases, as the proverb itself implies, the race is to the swift and the battle to the strong. And whether competition be considered under its best aspect or its worst, it is plain that, with such inequalities as now exist among men, the slow will generally be distanced by the swift and the weak beaten and trampled by the strong. If the law is that each shall grasp all that he can get, regardless of the welfare of his neighbor, it is evident that some will get much, and that many will get nothing.

"Competition," says Dr. Walker, "to have the beneficent effects which have been ascribed to it, must be all-pervading and unremitting, like the pressure of the atmosphere, of which we are happily unconscious because it is all the while equal within and without us, above and below us. Were that pressure to be made unequal, its effects would instantly become crushing and destructive. So it is with competition: when it becomes unequal, when the ability of one industrial class to respond to the impulses of self-interest is seriously reduced by ignorance, poverty, or whatever cause, while the classes with which it is to divide the product of industry are active, alert, mobile in a high degree, the most mischievous effects may be experienced." And again, after referring to those terrible injuries which the weaker classes often suffer through industrial disasters and depressions; to that physical and moral degradation into which whole populations are sometimes plunged, and out of which they can never rise without help from above themselves, the same strong writer goes on: "Such disasters aside, the tendency of purely economical forces [the tendency of competition] is continually to aggravate the disadvantages from which any person or class may suffer. The fact of being worsted in one conflict is an ill preparative for another encounter. Every gain which one party makes at the expense of another furnishes the sinews of war for further aggressions; every loss which one person or class of persons sustains in the competitions of industry weakens the capacity for future resistance. This principle applies with increasing force as men sink in the industrial scale." [1]

This is the actual working of those economic laws which have been depended on to bring the millennium. When we leave the airy heights of

[1] *The Wages Question*, pp. 163–165.

abstract economy and come down to actual life, this is what we find. If you want to know precisely what sort of fruit unrestricted competition will bring forth, study the history of English labor during the first quarter of this century. That was a time when "the economic forces" held undisputed sway. There were no laws to restrict freedom of contract; there were no trades-unions, or, if any timidly ventured into being, they were ruthlessly stamped out by the law; there was not much moral sentiment to restrain tyranny and extortion; supply and demand were the only regulative forces. That ought to have been a blessed season of peace and plenty for all. Was it so? For the capitalists it was; not for the laborers. Hear Mr. Thorold Rogers: "Children and women were worked for long hours in the mill, and the Arkwrights and Peels and a multitude more built up colossal fortunes on the misery of labor. . . . High profits were extracted from the labor of little children, and the race was stunted and starved, while mill-owners, land-owners, and stock-jobbers collected their millions from the toils of those whose wages they regulated and whose strength they exhausted."[1] Men, working sixteen or eighteen hours a day, earned in those desperate times from *a dollar and a quarter to a dollar and three quarters a week;* and the benumbing toil of little children brought their parents the merest pittance. About 1833, Mr. Hyndman tells us, "in good, well-managed factories around Manchester, the

[1] *Work and Wages*, p. 438.

labor of children had been reduced to eleven hours a day, but in return the period for meals had been shortened; whilst in Scotland and the north of England, twelve, thirteen, fourteen hours were still the rule for children. The ordinary age for children to go to factories was now nine years, but there were still many of five, six, and seven years old working in all parts of England. Nor was this unmeasured abuse of child labor confined to the cotton, silk, or wool industries. It spread in every direction. The profit was so great that nothing could stop its development. The report of 1842 is crammed with statements of the fearful overwork of girls and boys in iron and coal mines, which doubtless had been going on from the end of the eighteenth century. Children, being small and handy, were particularly convenient for small veins of coal and pits where no great amount of capital was embarked; they could get along where horses and mules could not. Little girls were forced to carry heavy baskets of coal up high ladders, and little girls and boys dragged the coal-bunkers along, instead of animals. Women were commonly employed underground at the filthiest tasks. In the iron mines, children of four to nine years old were dragged out of bed at four or five o'clock in the morning to undergo sixteen hours' work in the shafts, and if they faltered during their fearful labor were mercilessly flogged with leathern straps by the overseer."[1] These are

[1] *The Historical Basis of Socialism in England*, pp. 155, 156.

simply transcripts from the English government reports, and they are but part of a leaf out of volumes of horrors. It was to this that unrestricted competition brought the English laborer; and no economic force appeared for his deliverance, nor was there any sign of salvation coming to him from that quarter.

You may see something very like this in the condition of the sewing women of our own cities at the present time. This portion of the labor market is now economically "free." There is no law limiting the employment of women or protecting them from the greed of their employers; and there are no trades-unions, or none possessing much power, among these workers. The wages of sewing women are fixed by free contract; unrestricted competition rules in all this realm. The employers of these women are competing in the market for the sale of their goods. Each one is striving to undersell his competitors; the margin is narrow; the cost of material does not greatly vary; the only way that the cost of production can be lowered is by reducing the wages of labor. The more unscrupulous and hard-hearted of the employers, therefore, force down the wages; the rest are obliged to follow suit or lose the trade. Then the Shylocks give the screw another turn: what care they for the gaunt faces and the sunken eyes of the women by whose toil they seek to enrich themselves? Are they not bidden to buy their labor in the cheapest market? How can they tell when the minimum is reached?

They can tell only by experiment. As long as wages will go down, they will crowd them down. When these women are dead, others will be ready to sell their lives at the same price, — perhaps at a lower price. If they are driven to sell something dearer than life, what of that? Has ethics anything to do with economics? Thus it comes about — it is the logical consequence, the inevitable law — that the most rapacious employers fix the price of labor. When there is neither law, nor association of laborers, nor effective moral force to hold the "economic forces" in check, they always operate in this manner. Humane employers have nothing to say about the price of labor; if they do not follow the lead of the extortionists, they will be beaten in the competition and driven from the field. Women's wages in the productive industries are fixed by unrestricted competition, and they are quite generally starvation wages.

The same law operates in other departments. Listen to Mr. James Means, a shoe manufacturer of Massachusetts, talking to his men. He has been describing a season of good times and a subsequent gradual tightening of the market. "After a while, some fair-minded employers found out that some of their competitors were selling their products in the market just a little cheaper than they could possibly afford to sell. Those employers set about finding out the reason why those competitors were underselling them. What did they find? They found that some other employers, who were not fair-minded, had been cutting down the price of their labor, and thus, by reducing the price of their goods, were able to get away the trade from them. What could the fair-minded employers do about it? There were only two courses open to them. One was to close up their places of business and let their trade go away from them to those employers who had cut down their labor; the other was to cut down their pay-rolls to correspond with those of the employers who were grinding their employees. Were the fair-minded ones guilty of avarice? Not at all. They were perfectly helpless. . . . No matter how liberal-minded an employer may be, he cannot raise wages, because he has to sell his goods in competition with other employers who are crowding wages down. Those who are grinding their men can undersell him every time, and he must lose his business or cut down his pay-roll."

Such is the actual outcome of the unhindered working of the principle of competition. It results, no doubt, in a great cheapening of commodities, and in an equal cheapening of human life and human virtue; in the destruction of the weak, in the degradation of the ignorant, in the practical enslavement of the poor. True it is, as Professor Clark has said, that competition wholly without moral restraint has never existed. "If competition were supreme, it would be supremely unmoral; if it existed otherwise than by sufferance, it would be a demon. Nothing could be wilder or fiercer than an unrestricted struggle of millions of men for gain, and nothing more irrational than to present such a struggle as a scientific ideal."[1] But though, in spite of the theories of the individualistic economists, moral forces have interposed to check, to some extent, the savagery of this struggle, yet these moral influences have been so feeble, and those who sought to wield them have so often stood abashed in the presence of that false science which sought to banish them from the industrial domain, that their work has been ineffectually done; and the demon of individualism has had free range in society, with such consequences as we have seen.

Not laborers alone, but employers and capitalists as well, have found that competition, in the present state of human nature, is not an unmixed good. Not only does it crowd wages below the limit of subsistence; it also devours profits. Often by the fierceness of competition the gains of business are reduced to zero, and traders and manufacturers are forced to combine to save themselves from ruin. Combinations of capital are generally made for this purpose; it is not so much against the insurrection of labor that capital seeks to protect itself as against the foes of its own household. But when these combinations of employers are once made, they are found convenient in resisting the demands for higher wages, or in forcing reductions when the market is falling.

Such greedy and conscienceless reductions of

[1] *The Philosophy of Wealth*, p. 219.

wages as those which I have described lead necessarily to combinations of labor. It is the only thing that the wage-workers can do. If they suffer without resistance the operation of the economic forces, they will be degraded and destroyed; if they stand together for mutual protection, they may be saved. That brave and wise Massachusetts employer whose words to his men I have quoted sees this clearly. "You see," he says, "that the remedy cannot come from the employers; therefore, I say, it must come from those employed; therefore, I declare that the remedy must come from the organization of labor in trades-unions, for labor must be its own champion and right its own wrongs, and labor must combine and see to it that its power to purchase its own products is not taken away from it."

One of the largest employers of labor in my own city, Mr. Charles Lindenberg, thus expresses himself: —

"The employer, who in many cases is disposed to divide more justly with labor, is handicapped by competition. If I divide half of my profits with my employees, then my competitor can undersell me to this extent and make as much money as I do. While there may not be as much force in this objection as appears on the surface, yet the objection is an influential one in these times of sharp competition and narrow margins. To place all upon the same level and to overcome the general cupidity, the employer must be aided in his desire to do justice to the laborer by a more potent force than public opinion. Government, controlled by political parties, does not supply this power. The laborers themselves must create it by well-directed mutual effort, by combination within the law."

If all employers were like these two, there would be no serious labor question. The justice of their conclusions cannot be disputed. No dictate of prudence or of humanity is more obvious. In the absence of such combinations as they advocate, the fate of the wage-workers would be what it was in England sixty years ago, and what it is to-day among our working-women. If the wage system is to continue, labor must organize to save itself from extermination.

As a matter of fact, organization has brought deliverance to the laborer. From that deep degradation into which unhindered competition plunged the English laboring classes they have lifted themselves by combination. Not altogether without the aid of others have they wrought out this deliverance. The acts of Parliament, permitting and encouraging them to combine for their own protection, and all those bright chapters of factory legislation designed for their protection, were in large measure the work of men in other callings, who remembered the wage-slave in his bonds of penury as bound with him, and stooped to loose his chains. It was thus by the intervention of moral forces that succor was first brought to him. Armed with the right of combination, the English laborer has steadily regained the ground which he had lost, and his condition to-day is vastly better than it was fifty years ago. As a testimony respecting the effect of this method upon the welfare of the English laborer, let me quote a few sentences from the most eminent authority upon this subject, Mr. Thorold Rogers: —

"Three processes have been adopted by the working classes, each of which has had a vast, and should have an increasing influence in bettering the condition of labor. . . . They should be viewed by statesmen with unqualified favor, and be treated by workingmen as the instruments by which they can regain and consolidate the best interests of labor. They are: trade-unionism, or, as I prefer to call it, labor partnership; coöperation, or the combination in the same individuals of the functions of labor and capital; and benefit associations, or the machinery of a mutual assurance society. So important do I conceive these aids to the material, intellectual, and moral elevation of the working classes to be that I would, even at the risk of being thought reactionary, limit the privileges of citizenship, the franchise, parliamentary and local, to those, and those only, who entered into these three guilds, — the guild of labor, the guild of production and trade, and the guild of mutual help."[1]

Such testimony from an aristocrat, a Member of Parliament, and a Professor of Economic Science

[1] *Work and Wages*, p. 440.

in Oxford University, should be entitled to some weight. "When the working classes combine for the protection of their own labor against the effects of unrestrained competition, they are simply taking that course which is recommended alike by reason and experience."[1] So says the Duke of Argyll, one of the greatest of British aristocrats and landlords.

Thus it is that combination has been gradually supplanting competition. The hardships arising under unchecked competition became intolerable; capitalists on their side and workmen on theirs have been driven to combine for mutual protection. The great railroad companies, the great manufacturing interests, compete but imperfectly; they seek to combine. The workmen of most trades are organized in trades-unions; the unions are seeking an industrial federation; the Knights of Labor are ambitious to include and represent them all. What competition might do if it were free is now a question of speculative interest mainly; the question of the hour is rather what combination will do. To the philanthropic observer it sometimes appears that the strengthening of these organizations, on both sides, bodes no good to society. It looks like the realization in sociology of the physical paradox, — the collision of an irresistible force with an immovable body. But perhaps the result may be similar to that which science bids fair to achieve in naval warfare, when it seeks

[1] *The Reign of Law*, p. 373.

to construct guns that will pierce any armor, and armor that will resist any projectile. Under such circumstances naval warfare becomes impossible and absurd; we are forced to substitute reason and persuasion for steel and gunpowder. And it may be that the strengthening of the combinations of labor and capital for their conflict with each other will, in the same way, put an end to conflict. In the words of Professor Clark: —

"As the growth of a great corporation, absorbing all small establishments in a locality, suppresses competition among employers, the growth of a well-organized trades-union suppresses it among workmen. If both processes were consummated, and one corporation produced the entire supply of a particular article, while a trades-union controlled the entire labor force available for its production, actual competition would be at an end, and the division of the product would be affected by a bargaining process untempered by any of the conservative influences by which, in an open market, contracts are actually made. There would be no alternative buyers and sellers; the laborers would be compelled to sell their share of the product to the one corporate employer, and that employer would be compelled to buy the product of the trades-union, which, in a sense, is a single corporate laborer. The adjustment, if left to be effected by crude force, would produce disturbances too disastrous to be tolerated, and arbitration on a comprehensive scale would be a prime necessity. This condition is, as yet, only approximated. The solidarity of labor and capital is very incomplete. Corporations have not become absolute monopolies in their respective fields; trades-unions do not include all workmen. The bargaining process between capital and labor is not the blind and desperate struggle that it might be. It is tending toward that condition, and becoming, in a corresponding degree, dependent on arbitration." [1]

The statistics of strikes and lockouts collected by the National Labor Bureau showed that in the seven years from 1881 to 1886 there were, in the United States, 3,902 strikes, involving 22,304 establishments. The number of employees striking and involved was 1,323,203. Of lockouts during the same period, there were 2,214, and of employees locked out, 160,823. The loss to the men for this period of seven years was about $60,000,000, and to employers about $35,000,000. Of the strikes, a little more than 60 per cent. were wholly or partly successful, and a little less than 40 per cent. failed of their object. In England, the losses from strikes and lockouts for a term of ten years averaged about the same figure as in this country, — something like $15,000,000 a year. The pecuniary damage is serious; but the moral injury is far greater. It would seem that some remedy for these devastations ought to be found in Christian civilization.

The industrial revolution through which we have been passing may be roughly sketched and characterized in a few words: —

[1] *The Philosophy of Wealth*, pp. 136, 137.

1. The division of labor and the increase of machinery require, for the most efficient production, the large system of industry, with great aggregations of capital.

2. Under this system there is a tendency to the spoliation and degradation of the wage laborer.

3. To resist this tendency, labor combines, and ought to combine. Such combinations of labor may be abused; the men belonging to them may make gross blunders and unjust exactions; they are very likely to do so. Nevertheless, the organization of labor is necessary, under a wage system, to the preservation of the laboring class and to the welfare of society.

4. The right to belong to such an organization and the right to refuse to join it are equally sacred and inalienable. The employer who refuses to employ men because they belong to a trades-union, and the workmen who seek to prevent men from procuring employment because they do not belong to a trades-union, are equally unjust and equally tyrannical.

5. Such combinations of labor involve the right to strike for the increase or against the reduction of wages, or to secure any reasonable amelioration in the conditions of labor. If the employer or the company has the right to refuse to pay more than a certain wage, the employees have a right, individually or collectively, to refuse to work for less than a certain wage. The right to strike involves, however, no right on the part of the strikers to use vio-

lence toward their employer or their fellow-workmen who will not join them.

6. Strikes and lockouts are, however, methods of coercion, and ought to be the last resort. The employer who locks out his workmen because they will not take the reduced wage that he offers, and the workmen who strike because their employer will not give the increased wage that they demand, are both endeavoring to carry their point by inflicting injury upon their adversary. This involves the suffering of injury themselves; the question simply is, which can the longer endure the hardship. A most unsocial proceeding, assuredly: reason has no part in it; it is the essence of unreason.

7. The final function of these combinations must therefore be, not war, but arbitration. Arbitration can never take place until the workmen have learned to stand together; and it will never be admitted by the employers until these bands of workmen have shown themselves formidable. Strong combinations on the side of labor are the necessary conditions of arbitration. Capital will not arbitrate with a foe that it can crush. But when the antagonists are fairly matched, and it is evident that conflict can never take place without disaster to both, the voice of reason is more likely to be heard.

Arbitration is, then, the final term of the wage system. Unrestricted competition has practically broken down; combination for fighting purposes is simple brutishness, and cannot endure; the appeal to reason is the last resort. Is it possible to settle these labor disputes by this method? Can these great organized forces of capital and labor, now arrayed against each other, learn to confer on friendly terms and adjust their differences?

The first condition of successful arbitration is an unreserved and ungrudging admission on the part of employers of the right of the men to combine, and a clear recognition of the fact that the men stand upon an equal footing with themselves in the whole negotiation. It is very hard for many employers to recognize this right of the laborers to combine. The fact that these combinations of laborers often misuse their power; that they make unreasonable and injurious demands, and strike for foolish reasons, and sometimes resort to violence, is not to be denied. But if the abuse of privilege is a reason for the refusal of privilege, the right of capital to combine might, I think, be seriously questioned. Have we never heard of companies and corporations using their power selfishly and tyrannically? Even on the score of violence and turbulent lawlessness, it is by no means clear that the corporations and the capitalists are not as great sinners as the labor organizations. In two papers lying on my table while I was writing this page were illustrative items. The first was headed, "A Bloody Battle Fought in Pennsylvania over the Possession of a Mine." Two companies claimed possession of a mine; each armed its retainers, and, in the words of the dispatch, "a regular pitched battle was the result, during which a man named Sterling was severely beaten over the head, and probably fatally injured. Several others on both sides were badly hurt by the thrown stones." The second item, in the same day's paper, of the murder of a boy by the Pinkerton men at Jersey City, adds another to the list of such homicides for which capital is responsible. Where is the great railroad corporation that has not, at one time or another, resorted to violence in the assertion of its claims? Not long ago, the Baltimore and Ohio Railroad Company and the Pennsylvania Railroad Company fought a battle, within the corporation of my own city, for the possession of a railroad track. Nobody was killed, I believe, but that was good luck rather than good-will. The cutting of telegraph wires, the tearing up of railroad tracks, and all such offenses against property, — are they not of very frequent occurrence? And, aside from this resort to brute force, the gigantic lawlessness of corporations in their nefarious assaults upon the very foundations of government; in the bribing of courts and legislators and councilmen; in the robbery, by the forms of law, of thousands of innocent investors; in the wrecking, by corrupt and even felonious methods, of great properties, — is not all this a too familiar tale? Yet it is the representatives of these great organizations of capital who think that labor ought not to be permitted to organize, because its organizations sometimes behave in a disorderly and lawless manner!

"An examination of our social history," says Professor Ely, "reveals the fact that the laborers have been guilty of no offense for which they could not find a precedent in the conduct of unscrupulous employers. . . . I myself have seen the property of one railway corporation seized by another without the slightest ground in right or justice, and it was so common and every-day an occurrence that it attracted little attention. I am not aware that in all the United States a single editor thought it worth while to publish an editorial about it."[1] And Professor Thorold Rogers bears his testimony also in stinging words: "The violence which has characterized the action of workingmen against those who abstain from their policy, compete against them for employment in a crisis, and, as they believe, selfishly profit by a process which they are too mean to assist, but from which they reap no small advantage, is indefensible and suicidal. But it has its parallel in the attitude of joint stock companies to interlopers, and in the devices by which traders have over and over again striven to ruin rivals who will not abide by trade customs, or even seek to be independent competitors against powerful agencies. I see no difference, beyond the fact that law allows them, between the rattening of a Sheffield saw-grinder and the expedients by which, in the committee rooms of the House of Commons, railway directors seek to extinguish competition schemes. Men who have not

[1] *The Labor Movement in America*, pp. 164, 165.

had the refinements of education, and who are not practiced in the arts of polite malignity, may be coarse and rude in the expedients which they adopt; but when the process is essentially the same, when the motive is practically identical, and the result is precisely equal, the manner is of no importance to the analyst of motives and conduct." [1]

If the abuse of power should forbid the organization of labor, much more should it forbid the organization of capital. And the real purposes which the workingmen seek to realize through their organizations are certainly quite as lawful and quite as useful to society at large as those which the capitalists seek to realize through their organizations.

It must be expected that labor organizations will sometimes make grave mistakes and impossible demands. Whenever they do, they must inevitably suffer the consequences of their rashness. It is only by this experience of suffering that they will learn wisdom. But they will be much less likely to rush into these passionate extravagances if their right of organization is fully conceded by their employers. I think that fully half of the trouble now existing between employers and workingmen arises from the refusal of employers to make this concession. The workingman regards this refusal as the denial of one of his most sacred rights, and I agree with him. When all the captains of industry are ready to take the position of Mr. James Means and Mr. Charles Lindenberg, as quoted above, there will be

[1] *Work and Wages,* pp. 403, 404.

fewer troubles to arbitrate, and a much better prospect of successful arbitration.

Not only must the employers recognize the workman's right to combine; they must recognize his perfect equality with themselves in the discussion of wages. "My men shall not dictate to me what wages I shall pay," says the employer. Certainly not. Arbitration is not dictation. And neither shall you, therefore, dictate to your men what wages they shall receive. The notion "that the employer is the superior, the employee an inferior; that it is the right of the former to determine, the duty of the latter to acquiesce," is, as Mr. Joseph D. Weeks has said, the cause of much friction. The employer, Mr. Weeks continues, often "refuses to discuss questions that arise in connection with wages or the details of employment, in the discussion of which the employee has an interest equally with the employer; or, if such discussions take place, they are 'permitted,' an interview is 'granted.' . . . The true relation of employer and employed is that of independent equals, uniting their efforts to a given end, each with the power, within certain limits, to determine his *own* rights, but not to prescribe the duties of the others."[1] This fact must be fully admitted before arbitration can bring forth its good fruits.

These methods of arbitration are applied to the prevention as well as the settlement of labor disputes. There are committees of conciliation, to

[1] *Labor Differences and their Settlement*, p. 10.

whom questions threatening conflict are referred, and by whom the difficulties are often composed before the open rupture occurs. There are also boards of arbitration, to which appeal is made for the decision of irreconcilable differences. I cannot here go into the history of these peaceful methods by which in France for almost a century, and in England for many years, the disputes of employers and employees have been obviated or healed, to the vast advantage of both parties. When it is asked whether arbitration is practicable, the verdict of experience is clear and emphatic. In France and Belgium the work is done by legal tribunals; in England voluntary arbitration has been the rule, and three of the great industries of that country, the hosiery trade, the manufactured-iron trade, and the coal mining in the northern districts, have been preserved for many years from serious difficulties.

What, now, is the precise question to be submitted, in each case, to arbitration? Let us suppose that a strike has occurred, and that the employers and the workingmen have agreed to submit the matter in dispute to arbitration. What is the matter in dispute? What question must these arbitrators answer? It is simply the question, "What is right and fair?" What wages ought this employer to pay his men? What profit ought these men to allow the employer on his capital, and what reward is he entitled to for his management of the business? It is right and fair for the employer to pay his men what he can afford to pay them, after reserving to himself a *reasonable* reward for his skill, his business experience, and the abstinence which has enabled him to accumulate his capital. It is not right and fair that he should be growing rich very rapidly by means of their labor, while they are living in penury. On the other hand, it is not right and fair that he should pay them a rate of wages which will deprive him of profits, or cripple the business, or leave him without adequate motive to undertake the labors, the risks, and the pinching economies that are involved in the accumulation of capital and the organization of labor. Thus the question before the arbitrators is always a question of justice. If they ask what the employer can afford to pay, and what the workingman can afford to take, the standard by which they must judge is a standard of reason or equity. It may be difficult to fix the standard; in many cases it surely will be; but that must be their endeavor. It is not a question for force to determine, for force has been laid aside. It is not what each *can* get, but what each *ought* to get. The whole controversy has been removed from the realm of natural law and physical force into the moral realm. This is precisely what arbitration signifies. It is the substitution of moral law for physical law in the distribution of the product of industry. *It is an attempt to moralize the relations of capital and labor.* Natural impulse has hitherto been relied upon to effect a proper distribution of wealth, and it has failed, not because it was too weak, but because it was too strong through the flesh; reason and judgment have been called in to take its place. Is not this a significant event in the history of civilization?

"This method," says Mr. Weeks, "takes cognizance of existing conditions; recognizes the perfect equality of employer and employed; commits the prevention and settlement of these differences to the reason and judgment of both, not to the selfish impulses of one; refuses to recognize force; does away with the necessity and excuse for strikes and lockouts; permits due weight to be given to economical forces, and due consideration to any action their presence and power demand; furnishes the nearest approach to a free open labor market that has yet been established; in a word, it meets better than any method yet proposed the conditions necessary to a satisfactory and intelligent discussion and settlement of these questions, and offers far greater security that justice will be done and equality and peace established than does any method that relies upon blind, unreasoning, undiscriminating law or force." [1]

Will the moral forces be found adequate to regulate this vast domain, so full of greed and deceit and violence? Will grasping employers on the one hand, and rude and turbulent workingmen on the other, submit to the rule of reason and justice? That there is reason for doubt and fear I do not conceal from myself, but there is also some reason

[1] *Labor Differences and their Settlement*, p. 38.

for hope. If we could only prevail upon these contending parties to try this way, they would surely find it more excellent. The effect of righteousness is peace. The moral forces will certainly rule more benignly than the unmoral forces. Men will submit to reason and justice more willingly than to power. And the result of arbitration when it has been fairly tried encourages us to look for greatly improved relations between the contending parties through the operation of this method. In the present juncture, with the forces gathering, and the battle-cries resounding, and the peace of society threatened by reasonless collisions between masters and men, it is the one word that should be most earnestly spoken. Every man who has a voice should urge it. The folly, the stupidity, the brutishness of trying to settle the disputes that arise in the division of the product of labor by strikes or lockouts, by industrial war with its wasting and destruction and violence, ought to be condemned by every humane and order-loving man. Tell these quarreling factions that they must not fight. Make them feel that the resort to coercion is a crime that will bring down upon them the reprobation of all just men; that they must learn how to settle their differences by reason; that the party which first offers to arbitrate gains by that act the sympathy of the public; that the party which refuses arbitration, or will not abide by a fair award, puts itself under the ban of civilized society.

"Arbitration," says Professor E. J. James, "has

the great advantage of subjecting the acts of the parties to it to the efficient and powerful control of an energetic public opinion. It recognizes indirectly what is too often overlooked, that the interests at stake are not merely those of the laborer and employer, but also those of the community at large. The latter has such a great stake in the contest that it cannot afford to stand idly by and permit the former to disturb society to its foundations, and destroy in their struggle the very conditions of sound economic progress." [1] This is the truth which we must emphasize. We must make this industrial dueling as infamous as the other sort of dueling now is in civilized society. We must create a public opinion which shall scourge with its censure the kindling of strife that cripples industry, breeds pauperism, and scatters broadcast the seeds of enmity and scorn.

It is evident that for the present, and for the immediate future, arbitration of labor disputes is the one practicable measure, and that its effectiveness depends largely on the generation of a public sentiment that shall demand it, and watch its operations, and give emphasis and applause to its just decisions. The general prevalence of it, as Professor Clark has said, "would mean a reign of law, rather than of force, and would mark an era in the moral evolution of society." [2] A reign of law rather than of force society has a right to require of these contending parties; and it is a good omen

[1] *The Labor Problem*, p. 65.

[2] *The Philosophy of Wealth*, p. 177.

that so many voices are heard from the ranks of labor and from the captains of industry responding heartily to this demand. "Down with the red flag!" cries a journeyman printer in Milwaukee. "When nations can settle their difficulties by arbitration, why cannot capital and labor do likewise?" "I am confident," writes an iron manufacturer of Wheeling, "that could the parties connected with our nail-mills have had a board of arbitration, or even a conference committee, or any method of bringing the moderate and conservative men of both sides together, a settlement could have been reached; saving the immense loss of wages, keeping the busy wheels of mills in operation, avoiding scenes of riot, maintaining the peace, giving food and comfort to many families that have been deprived of it, and keeping many a good man from intemperance and vice, the sequences of idleness." "Without reason there is no arbitration," writes the secretary of a miners' union, "and arbitration means a stop to those prolonged and ruinous struggles between employers and employees, a striking of hands across the bloody chasm. Arbitration proper is the missing link between capital and labor." How earnestly Mr. Powderly has preached the gospel of arbitration I do not need to tell.

With such witnesses testifying on every hand, and such harmonious tongues singing the praises of arbitration, we will trust that upon many, in our generation, is about to fall the blessing of the peacemakers.

VII.

COÖPERATION THE LOGIC OF CHRISTIANITY.

"SOCIETY may be established and exist permanently," says Dr. Mark Hopkins, "on two principles, that of competition and that of coöperation. The first has its advantages, and the evils of it are diminished as general intelligence is increased. Under it the evils of ignorance are felt pecuniarily, and intelligence is thus stimulated. . . . But the principle of coöperation is far higher, and its results would be better."

Dr. Hopkins is speaking here, not as a political economist, but as a moral philosopher. The coöperation to which he refers is not a method of industry, but a principle of social life. He says that while certain personal advantages may be gained by competing with our fellow-men for the prizes of life, it would be better if we would coöperate with them for mutual benefit.

It has generally been assumed by economists that competition is the only effective principle of human association; that men were made to compete; that competition is their normal relation; that the well-being of society depends upon this incessant contest, in which each one is striving to get a larger portion than his neighbor of the good things of this life.

Now we may admit, with Dr. Hopkins, that this principle of competition has its advantages. It makes men keen and strenuous; it sharpens their wits; it strengthens their wills; it develops their individuality. And we may also admit that any form of society from which the operation of this principle, or some form of this principle, was wholly excluded would be likely to fail in developing the self-respect and self-reliance which are essential to all high character. Yet I cannot quite agree with the statement that society may exist permanently on the basis of competition. We found some reasons, in the last chapter, for believing that a society in which the relations of men were all competitive would not be society at all. Strife and warfare would be constant. Every man's hand would be against his neighbor. Such a society never existed. There has always been a great deal of competition in the world, but there has always been some good measure of coöperation, also. Men have been striving with one another for certain ends, and they have also been combining with one another for certain ends; their contests divided them, but their mutual interests united them; the repulsions of self-interest have been balanced, and often overbalanced, by the attractions of sympathy and good-will. Men compete in their business relations; on the streets, their rivalries, even if honest and fair, are sharp and incessant; each is trying to get the lion's share. But they come together in the neighborhood, in the school, in the church, in the secret fraternity, in the literary or musical society, in the political party, and in other associations where their interests are no longer divergent, but common, where the good of each is seen to be the good of all, where they find their profit in combining; and thus they learn to think of one another and to care for one another, and the social sentiments and activities are healthily developed. The coöperative principle and habit is really the cement of society: competition develops individual powers; coöperation develops social relations. As society advances from barbarism to civilization, men compete less and coöperate more. The principle of competition is the law of the survival of the fittest; it is the law of plants and brutes and brutish men; but it is not the highest law of civilized society; another and higher principle, the principle of good-will, the principle of mutual help, begins at length to operate. The struggle for existence, as Mr. Fiske says, must go on in the lower regions of organic life; "but as a determining factor in the highest work of evolution, it will disappear" with the progress of the race.

This is precisely the end at which Christianity aims. Its work in society may be summed up largely in this statement: it seeks to strengthen the principle of coöperation among men, and to hold in check the principle of competition. "The Master," says the great expounder of evolution, "knew full well that the time was not yet ripe, — that he brought not peace, but a sword. But he preached that gospel of great joy which is by and by to be realized by toiling humanity; and he announced ethical principles fit for the time that is to come."[1]

If, then, in Christian lands, coöperation is gaining upon competition; if, as the years go by, men strive less and combine more, this is a proof that Christ is a true prophet and a wise law-giver. Every movement in this direction is a sign of the coming of his kingdom. To my own mind, the conclusive evidences of the truth of Christianity are found in the social movements of the world about me. I know that Christ is king of men, that his kingdom is the kingdom of the truth, because I see that he has laid down laws to which men must conform in every relation of life if they would be happy and prosperous and free. To make plain this truth to men, to show them that Christ is actually establishing his kingdom in this world, is one way — it seems to me a very effective way — of preaching Christ. Yet there are persons who will listen to such a presentation, and then lament that Christ is not preached. A man who had never seen any light save one feeble ray that came through a keyhole into the dungeon where he was confined might lament, if you took him out of doors at noonday, because you had deprived him of his vision of the light. So a man who knows

[1] *The Destiny of Man*, p. 106.

nothing of Christ except the glimmering beams of his beauty that find their way through the cracks and orifices of some theological system may feel himself bereft if you show him the Light of the World, shining with noonday splendor all over the field of modern history. But men who are in the habit of living out of doors can hardly be expected to adjust their vision to the optical infirmities of theological troglodytes.

Let us see, then, whether we can express in familiar and untechnical terms the message of Christianity to the men of to-day. What is the authoritative word of this Master to employers and employed?

1. Its first clear utterance is aptly conveyed in the terms of that remonstrance spoken by the great law-giver of Israel to the two Hebrews whom he found fighting: "Sirs, ye are brethren; why do ye wrong one to another?" That employers and workmen are members of one family, vitally and indissolubly bound together, and that controversy and strife between them are not only injurious, but unnatural, is the fact which it emphasizes. The divine Fatherhood implies the human brotherhood, and the law of love covers all the relations of human life. Not merely to the church, but to the human race as well, does the apostle's metaphor of the body apply, "Ye are members one of another." And it would be just as rational for the right hand and the left hand to fly at each other, and beat and bruise each other till one or the other was disabled,

as it is for employer and employed to fall into contention and controversy. This great truth of the absolute unity of human interests, which involves the impossibility that any social class should rise by depressing another social class, which implies that if one member of the social organism suffers all the other members must suffer with it, is the corner-stone of Christian ethics, of Christian social science. Very slowly does the world move toward the realization of this truth; it is but a small section of the Christian church, even, that comprehends it. The sects proceed upon the theory that rivalry, and not coöperation, is the basis on which neighboring churches coexist; if they should make their creeds correspond with their deeds, they would profess their faith, not in the communion of saints, but in the competition of saints. The suggestion that churches dwelling in the same neighborhood should govern themselves by the Christian law in their relations with one another is often sneered at by sectarian leaders as visionary and impractical. "That may come to pass in the millennium," it is said, "but you cannot make it work in our day." When the churches themselves thus flatly repudiate the Christian law, it is scarcely to be wondered at that the factories spurn it. Yet it is the law of the church and of the factory, a law which not merely rests on the authoritative word of Christ, but which can be abundantly verified by experience. Out of all the turmoil and confusion of centuries of competition steadily emerges this truth, that it is not by strife and warfare, but by unity and coöperation, that humanity advances. The way of welfare is the way of peace. History, as well as Christian morality, warns us that we cannot mount to power and happiness upon the ruin of our fellows. This law of the unity of human interests is not true because Christ taught it; he taught it because it is true. It is the fundamental fact of human society; any adequate induction of human experience will verify it. Men have doubted it, denied it, fought against it through all the ages, but the word standeth sure, and every generation that passes brings it into clearer light.

When Moses chid his contending countrymen, saying, "Sirs, ye are brethren; why do ye wrong one to another?" the one most deeply in the wrong thrust him away, saying, "Who made thee a ruler and a judge over us?" That has always been the answer of human brutality and aggressiveness whenever the fact of the brotherhood of man has been asserted. But every year brings us a little nearer to the recognition of this principle, and we shall see, by and by, that it governs the relations of men in industrial society as well as in the church, the family, and the state.

"Sirs, ye are brethren!" You cannot obliterate that fact. You cannot afford to ignore it. In all your strikes and your lockouts, your black-listing and your boycotting, your combinations of capital to hold labor down and of laborers to defy and coerce capital, remember that the law of your being is, not conflict, but coöperation, and that while you are fighting one another you are fighting against the stars in their courses, against the Ruler of the universe; that you are doing not only a wicked, but an absurd, an unnatural, a monstrous thing.

2. Christianity teaches that the employer and the employed are not only brethren, but that they are also partners in business. You think immediately of the counsels of Paul addressed to masters and servants. This, you will say, is the relation recognized by the Christian ethics. And surely masters and servants are not business partners. I do not forget these words, nor do I fail to remember that the servants to whom Paul is writing were bondservants or slaves, — not even employees, but chattels of their employers. It will not be claimed that this is the relation which Christianity intends to establish. That Christ and his apostles recognized slavery as existing, and did not set themselves against it to overthrow it by direct onset, is most true; but it will be readily admitted that they established principles of morality which inevitably undermined it, and that they sought to guide industrial society toward a very different form of organization from that which is involved in slavery. That very principle which we have just been studying, of the brotherhood of man, of the organic unity of society, is the logical antithesis of slavery. That the time must certainly arrive when this institution should pass away,

when the master should cease to be the owner of the workman, and the laborer should cease to be the chattel of the employer, was as certain as that the kingdom of God should come. This was part of what was meant by the coming of the kingdom of God, for which men were taught to pray.

To slavery and serfdom the wage system has succeeded. Shall we say that this is the final form of industrial society? This is by no means clear; for though Christianity may recognize the wage system as it recognized slavery, and may not only refuse to make war upon it, but may even endeavor to persuade both employers and employed to behave justly and kindly toward one another while in this relation, still I have no doubt that the logic of Christianity must lead on to a higher and more equitable relation between them than that which is established by the wage system.

It is not necessary to use any extravagant language with regard to the condition of the wage-laborer. We sometimes hear him called a slave, and doubtless this seems to those of us who know the degree of comfort and independence to which many of our workingmen in England and America have attained an exaggerated and even preposterous assertion. Yet the fact cannot be denied that the tendency of the wage system of competitive industry is to divorce the working class both from the land and from capital. And it is certain as fate that a working class thus practically separated from the land and from capital — having, as a rule, no possession or control of the natural resources of the earth or the instruments of industry — will be a dependent class.

That this is the tendency of the wage system can scarcely be doubted. This tendency was allowed free play, as we have seen, in England during the first part of this century, and the degradation of labor was horrible. It has been checked since that time, partly by the intervention of good-will in the form of the Factory Legislation, partly by the combination of the laborers themselves. Doubtless the labor organizations have been the more efficient cause. And it is a palpable fact that, under a competitive wage system, labor can preserve itself from practical enslavement only by the maintenance of a standing army. That, in effect, is exactly what the labor organizations amount to. They are the standing army of labor, maintained at great cost, to prevent the subjugation of labor by associated capital.

Now, I do not think that Christianity contemplates the maintenance of standing armies of any sort. Whatever the politicians and economists may mean, the advent of Christ meant "Peace on earth and good-will to men," and the coming of his kingdom is signalized by the beating of swords into plowshares and of spears into pruning-hooks. Therefore, I am sure that Christianity must have something better in store for us than a system which involves organized conflict. Therefore it seems probable that the immediate effect of

Christianity must be the modification of the wage system and the incorporation with it of certain elements which shall tend to identify more perfectly and obviously the interests of the employer and the employed. Some form of business partnership between capital and labor is the logical and natural result of the application of Christian principles to this department of human affairs.

In making this adjustment, it will not be necessary to trample on economic laws nor to ignore the facts of human nature. The employer who recognizes his workmen as partners in production simply recognizes a fact. His partners they surely are. No clear economic analysis can make anything else of them. "What is the nature of wages?" asks an economist of the old school, and answers thus: "A capitalist and some laborers enter into an agreement for the purpose of production. Of this product the capitalist is entitled to retain a certain share, and the laborers a certain share."[1] This is a clear statement, and it is the exact economic truth. The sooner we make our organizations of industry frankly conform to it, the sooner we shall have peace and plenty. It is quite useless to fight against facts.

The truth that economists derive from their analysis of production is, then, the same truth that the Christian moralist deduces from the law of Christ. That all producers are partners is the corollary of the doctrine of human brotherhood.

[1] *Quarterly Journal of Economics*, i. 234.

If all men are brethren, the relation of the workmen to the organizer of work cannot be permanently that of a slave and master, or of dependent and patron, but must be that of coöperation and partnership. This is the logic of Christianity. This is the ideal which Christian ethics lifts up before us. This is the result to which all the overturnings in human society are steadily leading on. And although, as I have said, Christianity never proposes any violent assault upon the existing social order, but counsels all men to behave as Christians, with whatever social machinery they may be called to work, yet it tends steadily and powerfully toward the purification of social ideals, and the reconstruction of society according to its own law.

A man may be a Christian who is a master or a slave, but the logic of Christianity is liberty. A man may be a Christian who is an aristocrat or a plebeian, but the logic of Christianity is democracy. A man may be a Christian who is a capitalist or a wage-laborer, but the logic of Christianity is coöperation.

That the outcome of evolution in the political sphere is democracy seems to be tolerably clear. Carlyle admitted it long ago, with many deplorings; the political soothsayers of the period find no other sign in their horoscope. Some of the foremost nations have reached that level already; the rest are following fast. That political power is to be widely distributed admits of no doubt.

Now, I submit that the political enfranchisement of the masses of the people implies and requires their industrial enfranchisement. To make men who have no rights in the soil of the nation, and no control of the capital of the nation, by their votes rulers of the nation, is a political absurdity. The men who rule the state must have some larger stake in the commonwealth than a day's stipend; else they will rule carelessly, and mayhap maliciously. Those who are endowed with political power must be allied in interest with those who control the material resources of the state. Peace and security can be found in no other path. Can any man who has ever taken the trouble to think of what is involved in government by the people entertain a doubt as to the truth of this proposition?

The fact that the working class is losing its hold upon the land is pretty obvious. The number of mechanics and operatives who own homes of their own is not increasing in the country at large. There are a few localities, like Philadelphia, where Building Associations have resulted in increasing the number of proprietors; but in the manufacturing communities generally this is not the case. The precariousness of employment and the frequent need of migrating in search of work makes the ownership of a home undesirable to the majority of mechanics and operatives. The great companies usually prefer to furnish tenements for their employees; then, if trouble arises, they can be evicted without ceremony. Some companies, it is true, pursue a more humane policy, and not only encourage, but assist their workmen in procuring homes. Still, taking the country through, it will be found that a constantly diminishing population of the wage-workers live in homes of their own.

To what extent it is true that the capital of the country is passing out of their hands I cannot say. The savings-banks do, indeed, show a considerable increase of deposits; the proportion of these savings belonging to wage-workers is not well known. My impression is that clerks, domestics, school-teachers, and professional people own a large share of them. There appears to be a tendency to separate more and more widely the capitalistic classes from the working classes. I fear that there is a growing sentiment among the working classes that the possession of capital in such small hoards as they are able to gather is not worth while. The whole socialistic spirit is, of course, averse to the accumulation of individual property; and even the labor organizations, when they are not avowedly socialistic, are inclined to cultivate a feeling of dependence on the union rather than on private resources. But the chief discouragement of saving has been the centralizing tendency in business. The large system of industry is more and more prevailing; and the opportunity of the small capitalist or the small manufacturer lessens year by year. Thirty years ago the wage-worker might hope, if he saved a few hundred dollars, to set up business for himself in a small way; that chance is steadily diminishing. The big fishes devour the little ones so speedily and so surely that such risks are not often taken.

For such reasons the wage-working class tends, under present conditions, to become a propertiless class; that ugly word, the proletariat, threatens to be incorporated into our common speech. It seems to me that such a class cannot safely be permitted to exist in a democracy. I do not believe that we can afford to have a large toiling population who own no property, and have no direct and conscious share in the capital of the country; who even regard their interests as separate from or hostile to those of the propertied classes. And it seems to me that some way must be found of identifying the interests of the people who do the work of the country with those of the people who hold the capital and direct the work. The logic of the Christian law must be frankly accepted, and the fact must be recognized that employer and employed are business partners.

To this complexion it must come at last. The only question is how we shall achieve this social readjustment. It may come as the issue of social conflicts and agrarian wars; it may come as political equality came, with garments rolled in blood; it may come, and ought to come, as the slowly ripening fruit of Christian sentiments in the hearts of employers and employed. To this end it is needful that all Christians, whether employers or employees, should understand the logic of Christianity, and be ready to find and follow the plain path of its principles.

That the law of Christ is the law of coöperation seems to me very plain. We are steadily traveling toward an industrial order which will identify the interests of employer and employed. How fast we shall go is a question of expediency. Doubtless we might go too rapidly. It is possible that there may be laborers in the field of the world to-day who are scarcely fit for freedom — to whom some sort of peonage would be the best regimen. The trouble on this score is that there is no class of persons, so far as I know, who are fit to be masters, — to whom the possession of such power over their fellow-men would not be a serious injury. That there are many other laborers who are only fit to be wage-receivers is undoubtedly true. They lack the mental and moral discipline which would qualify them for associative effort. But there are many, I am sure, who are ready to take some steps in this direction. What the first steps ought to be I shall try to make plain in the next chapter. But the one thing needful is to identify, as speedily as possible and as completely as possible, the interests of the men who do the work with those of the men who direct the work.

We have already in operation certain forms of coöperative industry. What is called industrial coöperation is, indeed, only a faint and partial application of the larger Christian principle. But it is good so far as it goes. It is a step in the right direction. It will lead those who practice it up to a point from which they may discern the broader applications of the law.

Coöperation is the method by which men combine their savings as capital, and their efforts as laborers, and their interests as consumers in trade or manufacture or banking. It is an attempt to bring a large number of men together and unite them on the basis of mutual interest and mutual help. Within the association thus formed there is no competition; the interests of all are identical. Between this group of men and other groups or other individuals there may be sharp competition and rivalry; it is here that the narrowness and partiality of the scheme discovers itself; but it is something to teach the members of this group to coöperate with one another.

The universal complaint of the laboring classes is that the organizers of business are getting the lion's share of the increasing wealth; that much goes to profits which ought to come to them in wages. "The merchants, the manufacturers, the bankers," they say, "are getting rich out of our labor, while we remain poor. Therefore let us be our own merchants, our own employers, our own bankers, and keep all the profits for ourselves." This is what is called coöperation.

In three countries of the old world this principle has been developed in three different directions. In Germany, the greatest success has been achieved in coöperative banking; in France, in coöperative manufacturing; in England, in coöperative merchandising.

The coöperative banking which has been so successful in Germany is similar in principle to the operations of the Building and Loan Associations in this country, which in Philadelphia and in other cities have been very popular and useful. In 1852, Herr Schulze of Delitzsch succeeded in organizing, in accordance with laws which he had himself been instrumental in securing, a little "credit union" in his own town; and from this small beginning great things have come. In 1877, there were in Germany 1,827 of these loan associations, with 1,000,000 members; they had $40,000,000 of capital, and transacted an annual business of about $155,000,000. Italy, Austria, Hungary, and Russia have all followed the example of Germany, and in these four countries there were, in 1889, no less than 3,623 such associations, employing a capital of $350,000,000.

In France, as I have said, the success of coöperation has been most marked in the line of production. Of purely coöperative industries there are a goodly number in France, — most of them small, but thrifty and successful. Thus, I find, in the city of Paris alone, not less than 74 coöperative societies, engaged in all sorts of industries, — printing, watchmaking, saddlery, baking, cab-driving, — with a total number of 4,920 associates, and a yearly aggregate of work done amounting to about

$10,600,000. But it is in that peculiar form of coöperation which is known as industrial partnership, or profit sharing, that the French have achieved such signal success. That will be considered in another place. But these various forms of partnership bid fair to work a peaceful and beneficent revolution in the industries of that thrifty nation, and to establish between the different orders of society relations of amity and solidarity of interest that will go farther toward keeping the peace than all that can be done by the armies of France or by her legislators. When the capitalists and workmen of any country are thus confederated in the pursuits of peaceful industry, society has a powerful security against insurrection and war. Accordingly, it appears that in Paris, where this industrial reorganization has made more progress than anywhere else, there seems to be less fear of popular outbreaks at the present time than in some of the provinces. When General Boulanger was making his theatrical demonstrations, a few years ago, in the rural districts, Paris was perfectly quiet; the newspapers all declared that in this once feverish capital the great agitator had no following at all. How much of this is due to the McAll Mission I do not know; quite a little of it, I suspect. But I also believe that the peaceful organization of industry, by which employers and workmen become business partners, has something to do with the greater sobriety and conservatism of the Parisian working people.

In England, also, something has been done in the way of coöperative industry. During a recent visit to London, I found two exhibitions in progress, of a very interesting character, showing the growth of this form of social organization. The first was at the house of the Earl of Aberdeen, under the auspices of the coöperative Aid Association, — an association formed to aid workingmen's coöperative societies. More than seventy of these societies exist in different parts of England; of these, thirty were represented by their work in this exhibition. Textile industries of various sorts, fustian, hosiery, worsted, were here represented; boots and shoes, padlocks, washing and wringing machines, watches, cigarettes, mats, portmanteaus, trunks and bags, cocoa and chocolate, are all manufactured by various coöperative societies, and printing, house-decorating, and other such industries are similarly organized. It is acknowledged that many of these associations are doing business in a small way, and that coöperative production in England is still in its infancy; but there were reported at that time 78 such organizations in England, with 22,480 members, a capital of $4,750,000, a business amounting to $9,000,000 a year, and a profit of $350,000, or seven and one half per cent. on the capital invested. Such is the infant industry of coöperative production in England; it seems to be a healthy infant, and bids fair to grow up. Lord Brassey, a nobleman who has accumulated a fortune as an employer of labor, made an address at this meeting, in which he pointed out the difficulties in the way of industrial coöperators, in the keen competition to which they were forced with great corporations and very able managers; but declared that these associations were working on sound principles, and said that he was glad to admit that there had been a certain amount of success. "An ideal social system," said this high-minded nobleman, "involves a more even distribution of resources; the coöperative movement tends to that result, and we wish it to advance and develop as it never has done before."

The other meeting to which I alluded took place in the Crystal Palace at Sydenham. It was the National Coöperative Festival, the first great exhibition which was held in England for the purpose of showing the extent of the work accomplished in the application of this principle to industry and trade. To prove that some popular interest was felt in this exhibition, I may remark that 27,169 persons were admitted to the Palace on the day of this festival. Not only from London, but from all over England came throngs of people to see the fruit that has grown on this fair tree of coöperation. To the coöperative workers here assembled came greetings from some of the most distinguished political economists of England, and from several of the great statesmen. Mr. Gladstone wrote: "I am certainly under the belief that coöperative supply for the working classes has been the instrument of very great advantage, social and moral as well as economical; that it has, on the one hand, husbanded their resources, and on the other confirmed the habit of thrift and the sense of self-reliance and independence. To an agency so powerful and beneficial I tender my warm acknowledgments, with my hope that it may be even more prosperous and efficient in the future than in the past. I regard coöperative production as having special uses of its own, and as, on the whole, in its principles, not less beneficial than coöperation for supply; but as more difficult of execution, and as requiring the most cautious scrutiny of means and ends in each particular case."

Mr. Holyoake, the historian of coöperation, made an address on this occasion in which he set forth, with temperate eloquence, the purposes and aims of coöperators. "We are no enemies," he said, "to capital. What we want is to get a moderate share of it into the hands of those who earn it. Labor cannot thrive without capital, nor can capital earn a penny without labor. Therefore, since both are needful to the production of profit, both should share it. . . . The doctrine we proclaim is that labor has the same right to a share of profit as capital has to its interest. The ordinary outcome of capitalism is seen in the sweating system. It gives to the workman the wages of misery, and leaves him to perish when it no longer needs his services. Many generous employers show more consideration, and often pay wages in full when they make no profit. This is Employer's Socialism, which is no more respectable than State Socialism, since it subjects those who accept it to the humiliation of existing by sufferance and charity. Coöperators object to live by charity. They make no complaint of the aggressiveness of capital, that means feebleness; they make no supplication for better treatment, that means helplessness; but they decline to depend for subsistence on the condescension of capitalists. They have found a better way. Here are to be seen the products of coöperative workshops, where workmen and workwomen employ their own capital, and loan what more they need at current rates of interest; and all the profit they make is equitably apportioned among those who earn it by brain or hand. We show their work to-day, and ask all honest purchasers to buy it. We make no war on property; we envy no man his riches. We ask no gifts from the wealthy. All we ask is custom. . . . We do not expect the principles we maintain to be accepted all at once. The millennium of capital came long ago; the millennium of labor is hardly yet in sight, and will come in ways unseen by us."

There are few Anglo-Saxons on either side of the sea who cannot sympathize with these manly words, and who will not send their best wishes after the men who are making this brave effort after industrial independence.

I have spoken of the societies of coöperative production which were represented in this festival by their handiwork, but these were only a fraction of the great company of English coöperators. In England, as I have said, the success of coöperation has been mainly in the line of storekeeping. How great that success is few Americans know. Such mammoth establishments as the Rochdale Equitable Pioneers, with a membership of 11,161 persons, with a capital of $1,730,000, with annual sales of $1,310,000; and a net profit of something like $2,000,000; the Leeds Industrial, with annual sales of about $2,500,000; Oldham, with annual sales of $1,600,000; Bolton, with annual sales of nearly $1,500,000, and many others, show the extent to which coöperative distribution is carried in England. Thirteen such societies are named in a table before me, the annual business of each of which exceeds $1,000,000. There is a Great Coöperative Wholesale Society, which supplies these various local stores, and which in 1883 did a business amounting to more than $20,000,000.

Let me sum up this statistical statement by giving you the footings as presented at the Crystal Palace festival. These include both kinds of societies, the productive and the distributive. Of these societies, there are in the United Kingdom 1,281, with 833,811 members. In 1887, the business done by these bodies was represented by $155,000,000, while the profits were $14,800,000; the capital invested was more than $55,000,000, consequently the rate of profit was about twenty-five per cent. per annum.

In our own country, coöperation has been experimented with to some extent, and in some departments, as, for example, in the Coöperative Building and Loan Associations, with considerable success. In 1888, Mr. F. B. Sanborn reported that there were at least 3,000, perhaps 3,500, such associations in this country; that the loanable capital in their hands at any given time must be at least $300,000,000; and that the property accumulated by the aid of these associations within the last forty years was from $500,000,000 to $750,000,000. Coöperative production has had but scant opportunity in this country to prove its practicability. Dr. Albert Shaw has told an interesting and instructive story of the success of certain coöperative coopers in Minneapolis; and Dr. E. W. Bemis has carefully compiled the facts concerning coöperation in New England. Many such enterprises have been set on foot and abandoned; but Dr. Bemis gives the statistics of twenty coöperative factories doing business in New England in 1886, with an aggregate membership of 1,215, and an aggregate product of $738,000. In distributive coöperation the success has been much more marked. The figures of Dr. Bemis give us information respecting fifty-three coöperative stores, with 5,470 shareholders, and an annual trade of $1,609,401. And putting together all the kinds of coöperation, factories, creameries, stores, and banks, he concludes that the coöperative business of New England must have amounted in 1887 to $7,000,000.

Leaving out of sight the Coöperative Building

Associations, these figures are small when compared with the totals for Old England. I am not quite able to explain the meagre results of these coöperative experiments in America. Perhaps they may be due to the fact that the working class in this country has hitherto been less sharply differentiated from the other classes, is therefore less accustomed to stand together for the protection of its interest, and therefore less able to combine in industry and trade.

By this form of industrial coöperation the functions of labor and capital are combined: the laborers are the capitalists; the function of the *entrepreneur*, or undertaker, is eliminated; every laborer is also a capitalist; every workingman is his own employer. Professor Marshall says that "the ideal which the founders of the coöperative movement had before them was that of regenerating the world by restraining the cruel force of competition and substituting for it brotherly trust and coöperation. They saw that, under the sway of competition, much of men's energy is wasted in the endeavor to overreach one another. They saw the seller, whether of commodities or labor, striving to give as little, and that of as poor a quality, as he could. And they saw the buyer always trying to take advantage of the seller's necessity, and thus forcing the seller, and especially the seller of labor, to struggle against a reduction of price, even when, if the buyer were more open with him, he might see that the reduction was necessary. The

'Coöperative Faith' is rather felt than clearly expressed, but it is earnestly held by shrewd practical men. It is that these evils can be in a great measure removed by that spirit of brotherly trust and openness which, though undeveloped, is yet latent in man's nature. It looks forward to a time when man shall have so far progressed that there shall be no needless secrecy in business, and each one shall think of promoting the general well-being as much as of protecting his own interests. Thus, its ultimate aim has a resemblance to that which prevailed in the early Christian church, and which led them to a community of goods. Coöperation is divided from most modern socialistic schemes by advocating no disturbance of private property, by insisting on self-help, and by abhorring state help and all unnecessary interference with individual freedom." [1]

This ideal is one that we can well afford to cherish. Under the present industrial system, in which machinery plays so large a part, if the laborer cannot achieve something like this, it is difficult to see how he can permanently improve his condition. For the law of the universe, a law that no man and no social system can greatly obstruct in its working, has ordained that intelligence shall be victor over mere force. Now, in a great and constantly increasing majority of the industrial operations of the present day, the intelligence is mainly embodied in the machine: the machine does the

[1] *Economics of Industry*, p. 219.

thinking; the machine is crystallized intelligence of the highest and finest quality. The man who tends the machine has very little thinking to do; his actions are largely automatic.[1] Therefore, by the law of the universe, the machine, or the man who owns it, will take the largest share of the product. It is useless to kick against this law; it will get itself enforced in the long run in spite of us. If the laborer wishes materially to improve his condition, he must own the machine. How is he going to get it? That is a very hard question. In some peaceful and reasonable way, I trust. He must not think of stealing it or of taking it by violence; when he does that, he runs against another law of the universe which will destroy him. The only present prospect of his getting it lies in his learning to work and wait and save till he can possess it honestly.

He will need, too, something besides the machinery: he will need a trained intelligence, a knowledge of trade, a technical skill, an educated taste, a grasp of affairs, that are not gained in a day; without these he will never be able to operate his machinery successfully. Industry must, in these latter days, be conducted on the large system; many workmen will be compelled to combine, with their machines and their savings; and unless they are, collectively, as competent to manage a great business as the ablest of our modern captains of industry, and unless they can agree as

[1] *Microcosms*, ii. 388.

to methods and measures, which of course is too much to hope for, they will be obliged to choose some one who has the requisite business qualities, and commit the management to him, and pay him liberally for this service. To unite thus in the choice of a leader, and to coöperate with him and with one another, requires a high degree of intelligence and self-control. The patience and frugality which can accumulate the necessary capital, and the judgment and moderation and sweet reasonableness which can harmoniously and successfully direct the management of it in a great manufacturing industry, are not so common among workingmen as they will be one day. Where they do not exist, coöperation can never be successful. It is the lack of these qualities that explains the failure of many of the coöperative experiments. Truly has it been said that large success in coöperation must await "the development of the coöperative man." And yet there is some reason to hope, with Dr. Albert Shaw, "that all conditions are favorable to his development, and that his advent will be a realized fact almost before we are aware of it." What chiefly hinders this is the preoccupation of the mind of the wage-worker with the business of maintaining war against capitalists and employers. The workingmen have expended a great deal of time and energy and money, during the last twenty-five years, in efforts designed to wrest from the managers of business a larger share of the product. Some of this expenditure was necessary, no doubt; but if they had given a good portion of it to the accumulation of capital, and the equipment of themselves for the control of productive industries, they would be a great deal better off than they are to-day.

It is probable, however, as I shall try to show farther on, that for a great majority of the workmen now at work industrial partnership or profit sharing would be a safer and more profitable method than pure coöperation. The captain of industry who will make them partners with himself in sharing the gains of industry can, in most cases, with his intelligence, his business experience, and his executive energy, organize and direct their labor in such a way as to realize from it, in wages and added profits, a larger reward for laborers than they could gain by any combinations of their own. If, under such leadership, they will make the most of their opportunities, and save their earnings, and train themselves and their children to studious, sober, industrious ways of living, using for purposes of self-improvement the enlarged leisure that must come to them through the marvelous improvement of the power of machinery, they will greatly hasten "the development of the coöperative man," and the coming of that kingdom of peaceful industry of which he will be the ruler.

VIII.

THE REORGANIZATION OF INDUSTRY.

In a previous chapter we traced the industrial revolution through the collapse of unrestricted competition to the rise of combination, and studied the method of arbitration as a means of adjusting labor disputes. That arbitration is the word of the hour is clear enough; that it is the last word of the answer to the labor question is not probable. For the wage system arbitration is indispensable; but we found good reason in the last chapter for hoping that there is something better in store for the laboring millions than the wage system could promise them.

An intelligent capitalist employer in the West takes this philosophical view of the matter: "Arbitration is not a panacea to cure the ills of labor, but it represents the next stage of human development in advance of strikes. In the Middle Ages might was right, and every dispute was settled by a resort to force. This was the age of feudalism. Following that came the establishment of courts of justice for the settlement of disputes, and the judge and lawyer took the place of the baron and soldier in the settlement of private differences. Strikes and lockouts are the characteristics of the feudal age of labor and capital, and arbitration will be the characteristic of the age of law. But arbitration will probably bring no greater satisfaction for either side. It will merely involve the use of different and less costly and more humane methods, and hence it means one step in advance." [1] If arbitration uses less costly and more humane methods, it ought to bring some satisfaction to both sides. But the fact that it furnishes only a partial solution to this great problem is not to be concealed.

Professor Henry C. Adams offers this opinion: "Arbitration is not the missing coupling between capital and labor, but is the thing for which, at the present time, it is practical that workingmen should strive. Its establishment is the first step toward the overthrow of the wages system." [2] And Professor Clark, in that admirable little book from which I have so often quoted, makes this statement: "The general prevalence of [arbitration] would mean a reign of law rather than of force, and would mark an era in the moral evolution of society. The era would, however, be one of quasi-litigation. To be successful, the plan of arbitration requires many tribunals in ceaseless activity. It checks lockouts and strikes, and allays the antagonisms excited by these overt conflicts. The speedy establishment of these tribunals is, therefore, the present desideratum. Yet the arbitrative system is not an ideal one. Its fundamental defect lies in the fact that

[1] *The Labor Problem*, p. 91. [2] *Ibid.* p. 62.

it concentrates the attention of employers and of workmen upon the terms of the division of their joint product. An issue of this kind, even if amicably adjusted, tends in itself in the direction of antagonism. It fails, moreover, to secure the largest product for division."[1]

Under the wage system there is a natural and irrepressible conflict between the employer and his employees. It has been a common saying — we have all said it scores of times — that there is perfect identity of interest between the workmen and their employer. This is what ought to be; but it is not what the wage system gives us. Under this system, as some one has said, their interests are no more identical than the interests of the buyer and the seller. They are alike interested in the work of production, in making the product as large as possible; when the division of the product comes to be made, the interest of the one party is antagonistic to that of the other. The more the master gets, the less the men will get. The gains of production, after rent is deducted, are shared between those who have made them: one part goes to the capitalist-employer as interest on capital and earnings of management; the other part goes to the laborers as wages. The larger the one share is, the smaller the other must be. If there is a definite quantity of commodities to be divided between you and me, I shall find it quite impossible to convince you that it makes no difference to you how much I

[1] *The Philosophy of Wealth*, p. 178.

take. Of spiritual possessions it is true, that the more you part with the more you have left; but it is not true of material things. In the distribution of the wealth produced, masters and men are not one, but twain. Arbitration tries to temper the inevitable strife; to keep the parties from fighting over the spoils; to persuade them to use reason rather than force in making the division. But this is a difficult task; it is often hard to convince one of the parties that the other has not obtained an unfair share of the common gain. The diversity of interest keeps industrial society in unstable equilibrium. It is a great gain when men learn to apply moral standards to this problem, — to ask what they ought to have, rather than what they can extort; nevertheless, the clamors of self-interest will be loud and incessant, and the moral judgment will sometimes fail to get a candid hearing. This is a very unfortunate condition of things, and men of good-will are constantly constrained to ask whether some adjustment of the relations between the employer and the laborer might not be made, by which their interests should become, in some greater measure, harmonious, if not identical. This is what is proposed in the scheme of industrial partnership or profit sharing, which is destined, we may hope, to form the next stage in the industrial evolution. This plan recognizes a limited partnership between the employer and the employed, and provides that wages shall vary with profits, rising as they rise, and falling as they fall.

It is an admission that the workingman has an interest in the business; that the contract by which he receives a certain wage does not express his whole relation to the business; that it is conducted, not exclusively for the benefit of the employer, but also for the benefit of the laborer. Instead of implying, as the strictly competitive system implies, that the employer will give his men the least share of their joint product that he can compel them to take, it implies that the employer will give his men the largest share of the product that he can afford to give. It is an announcement that the manager of the business intends that his helpers of all grades shall reap with himself the benefits of any prosperous fortunes that may overtake the enterprise, while they bear with him the burdens of the unprosperous years.

This last point needs to be emphasized at the outset; because it is the one stereotyped objection to the plan, that it makes the workmen sharers in the profits and not in the losses. That, indeed, would be a serious objection if it were well grounded; but the fact that it is urged shows how superficially the objectors have studied the plan. Of the hundreds of industrial establishments now working on this basis, there are few which do not, expressly or tacitly, recognize the fact that the workmen must share in the losses as well as in the gains. It is the phrase "profit sharing," probably, over which these rather careless critics have stumbled. For this reason, it is better to use the other designation. "Industrial partnership" is a more descriptive name for the system.

Under this system, the capital is furnished and the business is organized and directed by the employer: the workmen are paid wages at the market rate, and at the end of the year a stipulated percentage of the net profits is divided among them, each man's dividend being proportioned to the amount of his earnings. Usually it is agreed that those only are to receive the dividend who have been in the service a certain length of time, and that workmen discharged for cause are not entitled to a share in this fund.

This plan makes the workmen partners in the business; they are not merely "hands," they are associates; their eyes and their brains and their hearts are enlisted as well as their hands; their interests are identified with those of the employer; the larger the gains of the business are, the larger their share will be.

"Suppose that there are no gains," one may query. "Suppose what often happens, that the business makes no net profit during the year." Then, of course, there will be nothing to divide. The workmen will have had their wages, all that they would have had under the old system, but they will get no bonus at the end of the year.

"But suppose there are losses, instead of profits," the querist urges. "Such seasons occur in most industries." Undoubtedly; and the system should provide for these by setting aside, at the end of every prosperous year, a certain share of the profits as a reserve fund, to keep the capital good in the unprosperous years. This reserve fund should always be set aside before the dividend to labor is made. Thus the workmen are made to share in the losses as well as in the gains of the business; their dividends are diminished in the good years that their wages may be paid in the bad years. It would not be difficult to make the average workingman see the reason of this provision and feel the justice of it; it will be found, on experiment, that the average American workingman will behave in a very considerate and manly way when any attempt is made by his employer to take him into confidence with regard to matters of this nature.

Let us suppose a case, which, as we shall shortly see, is the type of a large and constantly increasing class. An employer calls his men about him, at the beginning of the year, and thus addresses them: "This business is not mine exclusively; it is yours also. I contribute the materials, the machinery, the organizing and directing force; you do the work. I have paid you wages hitherto, at the market rate. I shall continue to pay you as much as similar workmen are receiving in other establishments. I will also pay myself a certain reasonable salary for managing the business; no more than I could earn as manager, if I chose to hire myself out to another man. At the end of the year, if we have made anything, I will set aside ten per cent. of the profits for a reserve fund; of all that is left, I will give you one third, dividing it among you in proportion to your several earnings. Thus, if the business clears thirty thousand dollars, I shall set aside three thousand dollars for a reserve fund, and there will be twenty-seven thousand dollars left. Of this your share will be nine thousand dollars. There are one hundred of you, and you will have, on an average, ninety dollars each. I am only imagining a case; the dividend may be much less than this, but your share, whatever it may be, I will pay you on the tenth day of January next. If we make no profits, you will have nothing but your wages, and I shall have nothing except my salary. The larger the profits of the business are, the larger your share will be. The more diligently you work, the more careful and economical you are in handling materials and tools, the larger will be the profit we shall have to divide. I promise to do my best to make your share as large as possible; I trust you will do as much for me."

What would be the probable result of such a proposition? Reasoning from what we know of human nature, is it not likely that it would be accepted by the workmen with gratitude; that it would establish at once a friendly instead of a suspicious and antipathetic relation between themselves and their employer; that it would render their labor more efficient, and result in much saving in the use of machinery and materials; and that, in many cases, the net profits would be so much increased through the increased efficiency and economy of labor that, after paying the workmen's share, the employer would have quite as much left as he would have had under the old arrangement?

On purely economical grounds, therefore, this method is justified. Whatever increases the efficiency of labor is beneficial both to the employer and to the employed; it increases the product to be divided between them. This is a principle which has not, indeed, always been recognized by economists; they sometimes reason about "labor" as if it were a constant force like gravitation, which can be neither increased nor diminished. This Adam Smith expressly says: "The productive powers of the same number of laborers cannot be increased but in consequence either of some addition and improvement to those machines and instruments which facilitate and abridge labor, or of a more proper division and distribution of employment."[1] It is this habit of reasoning about labor which has made much of the trouble. The laborer is not merely the embodiment of so many foot-pounds of muscular force; he is a human being, with hopes and fears, affections and ambitions; and the efficiency of his work, in the great majority of callings, greatly depends upon his state of mind. If his interest is thoroughly enlisted in the enterprise in which he is engaged, if his good-

[1] *The Wealth of Nations*, Book II. chap. iii.

will is called into exercise, his product may be largely increased. The obvious and painful fact is that the fierce and bitter conflict between the employing classes and the laborers has developed unsympathetic if not unfriendly relations between them. There are exceptional cases, but this is the rule. And this state of feeling affects production injuriously. A vast amount of poor, heartless, wasteful, slipshod work is due to this cause. And the employer who can succeed in establishing better relations between himself and his workmen will discover the benefits of this policy in the footings of his annual balance sheet.

What is of not less consequence, he will have peace and good-will between himself and his workmen, instead of suspicion and strife; he can make his contracts with confidence; he will feel well assured that he will not be interrupted by threats of a strike when the tide of business turns toward prosperity.

But even if gains should be somewhat lessened that the workmen's share might be increased, many employers would feel that the improvement in the circumstances of their men and the opening of a door of hope to them are benefits for which they would be willing to make some sacrifices. My own belief is that industrial partnership would prove, in almost all cases, a pecuniary advantage to the employer, but it would be a mistake to urge the measure on employers wholly or mainly on the ground of pecuniary advantage. This labor question will never be settled until employers as well as workmen form the habit of thinking of something besides their pecuniary advantage. I would seek to commend this scheme to the captains of industry by appealing to their humanity and their justice; by asking them to consider the welfare of their workmen as well as their own. I believe that these leaders of business are not devoid of chivalry; that they are ready to respond to the summons of good-will. Many of them are tired of the strife that is engendered by competition, and they would fain escape from that constant collision of interests which calls for arbitration; the promise of industrial peace is a welcome word to them; and the desire not only to live in amity with the men by whose labor they are seeking their fortunes, but to befriend and help them, is not always absent from their breasts. Materialistic economy sneers at sentiments of this sort as visionary and ineffective; the time is coming, I trust, when it will not be possible to leave them out of the account in our reckoning of the economic forces.

I have been speaking hypothetically, but there is small need of this, for the system of industrial partnership is no mere airy possibility; its wisdom and efficiency have been demonstrated by the happy and fruitful experience of many years in scores of industrial establishments of all sorts and sizes. The skepticism which is often expressed as to the practicability of this method is really a somewhat discreditable exposure of ignorance.

After a piece of machinery has been at work for twenty years, smoothly, successfully, productively, in a great many different hands and upon a great many kinds of material, making a finer product than was ever made before, it is rather ridiculous to hear a man who never tried it and never saw it volunteer his opinion that it will not work. I have frequently been visited with the contempt, and sometimes with the commiseration, of so-called practical men, when I have ventured to suggest this method; they were ready to dismiss it at once as the dream of a theorist. "What does a parson know," they wanted to ask, "about the management of business?" Waiving all dispute as to the parson's "practical" wisdom, he is as fully qualified as any other man to see and report a simple historical fact. He may not know how to run a steam-engine, but he may be perfectly sure that there are many thousands of steam-engines in operation in various parts of the world, and that they are doing good work. That I could manage a hundred workmen in an industrial partnership I will not assert; but I do know that the thing has been done by a great many other men, and that the testimony of those who have tried it is almost unanimous, and very enthusiastic in its favor.

A little book, published a few years ago in England by Mr. Sedley Taylor, contains much interesting information upon this subject. A much larger volume, lately published in this country by Mr. N. P. Gilman, greatly extends the information.

It is upon the continent of Europe that this method has been most thoroughly tried, and most of Mr. Taylor's and Mr. Gilman's facts are drawn from France and Germany. To show you at the outset how much had been done at the time when the first-named book was written, let me quote: "Putting together the most recent data, I shall be below the mark in saying that one hundred Continental firms are now working on a participatory basis. The principle has been introduced with good results into agriculture; into the administration of railways, banks, and insurance offices; into iron-smelting, type-founding, and cotton-spinning; into the manufacture of tools, paper, chemicals, lucifer matches, soap, cardboard, and cigarette-papers; into printing, engraving, cabinet-making, house-painting, and plumbing; into stock-broking, bookselling, the iron trade, and haberdashery. This list does not profess to be anything like complete, but it will probably suffice for the purpose now in view. The establishments which it summarizes differ in size and importance as much as in the character of the industry which they pursue, from the paper-mills of M. Larouche Joubert at Angouleme, with their fifteen hundred workmen, to the establishment of M. Lenoir at Paris, with its fifty house-painters. I may add that the movement is making decided headway, a considerable number of houses having given in their adhesion during the last four years."[1] This will indicate

[1] *Profit Sharing in Industry*, p. 39.

that the thing which I am talking about is not in the clouds nor in the vapory brains of a few half-crazed doctrinaires, but that it stands on solid ground and has .substantial results to exhibit. It shows, also, that the field in which this method has been put to the proof is already very broad; the notion that it is workable only in a few exceptional industries is pretty well discredited by these figures. One or two recent volumes undertake to show the impracticability of profit sharing; in one of them the surprising statement is made that seventy-five per cent. of such experiments have been failures. Mr. Gilman's treatise, which is a most careful and exhaustive presentation of the facts, gives complete reports of 135 such enterprises now in operation, and mentions twenty-one others of which full reports could not be obtained; while the total list of those in which profit sharing has been tried and abandoned is only 36, and in nine of these, according to the testimony of the firms themselves, the principle was successful; the abandonment of the experiment was due to no fault in the method. It would appear, therefore, that, so far as heard from, eighty-six per cent. of these enterprises have succeeded. A recent review of one of these hostile treatises concludes with the remark that the arguments of the book against the system are "the more impressive" because "the author is a Fabian Socialist, with a strong bias against the wage system, and in favor of some form of socialistic production." The innocence of this remark is engaging. It is much as if one should say of a temperance reformer, "His condemnation of High License is all the more impressive because he is known to be an ardent Prohibitionist." If there is any class of persons in the community who are consistently and resolutely skeptical about industrial partnership, it is the Socialists; not a few of the failures recorded in Mr. Gilman's book are traced directly to the determined hostility of revolutionary Socialists. In the words of Mr. Gilman, "The comparatively modest scheme of participation in simple profits stands little chance of impressing workmen favorably when their minds are filled with ideas of a universal division, or a common enjoyment of prosperity, under the name of Socialism." The feeling of the average Socialist, when profit sharing is proposed to him, is much like that of the Irishman just landed, who rebuked his friend for stooping to pick up a half-dollar on the wharf: "Tush, man, let it alone; a little beyant here ye 'll shovel 'em up." In audiences to which I have sought to commend this method of industry, I have invariably found Socialists the most unsympathetic listeners; they are quite apt to get up and stalk out of the house. The reason of this is, of course, their conviction that this simple remedy is ineffectual. Doubtless they are honest in this conviction, but their feelings are too much enlisted; they are not, as a rule, in a judicial frame of mind. The testimony of Socialist writers concerning the failure of profit sharing enterprises is always to be taken with much caution.

Mr. Macleod undertakes to show that there are two kinds of labor in commerce, one of which is necessary to produce the profit, the other of which is not. "In a merchant's office," he says, "or in a bank, the clerks, servants, messengers, porters, etc., contribute nothing to the success of the business. Such labor as theirs is subject to the simple rule of Demand and Supply. They have no shadow of a claim to demand a share of the profits. . . . So the servants of a railway company, engine-drivers, guards, porters, and clerks, contribute nothing to the success of the enterprise. . . . But the labor of operatives, miners, and artisans stands on a different footing altogether. Their labor, their skill, is indispensably necessary, and conduces directly to obtain the product and the profit. Their labor may justly be styled coöperative with that of the master; they are in reality quasi-partners with the capitalist in obtaining the profits, and without them the profits could not be made, and the master obtains a distinct profit out of the labor of such workmen which he can estimate in a very different sense to that of the labor of the other class. It is now pretty generally recognized that such workmen have an equitable claim to a certain share of the profit which is the result of the joint efforts of the master and workmen."[1] The admissions of the last part of this

[1] *Elements of Economics*, ii. 204, 205.

quotation are significant. That the labor of *some* laborers is "coöperative with that of the master," and that "they are in reality quasi-partners with the capitalist in obtaining the profits," is a somewhat belated discovery of this school of economists; it ought to have a good deal of practical influence upon the distribution of wealth. The only weakness of this reasoning is the attempt to show that this principle holds in some industries, and not in others. Mr. Macleod asserts that in mercantile and financial operations the success of the business depends in no degree upon the employees. As a matter of fact, this method has been in use for a long time in mercantile houses; the remuneration of salesmen is generally conditioned in part upon the amount of their sales. Perhaps, however, Mr. Macleod did not intend to include salesmen among clerks. But the inaccuracy of what he says about financial houses is illustrated by one of the most conspicuous instances of industrial partnership, that of a great insurance company of Paris, which has now for forty years divided a portion of its earnings among the whole number of its employees of all grades, and which, up to 1885, had collected and distributed more than a million and a half of dollars in this way, in addition to the regular salaries and wages of its men. Bookkeepers, clerks, and all other servants of the company share in this dividend in proportion to their earnings, and the president of the company, M. de Courcy, wrote in 1880 to Mr. Taylor: —

"Each year the company appreciates better what it gains in return for these sacrifices. My general principle is that there are no thoroughly satisfactory business transactions except those which are satisfactory to both the parties concerned. Experience has justified our institution from both these points of view. It is excellent for the employees and excellent for the company." [1]

This experience of forty years may, perhaps, outweigh Mr. Macleod's dictum about the inapplicability of this principle to financial houses. Mr. Gilman reports thirteen insurance and banking houses which are doing business by this method. What Mr. Macleod says about railway employees is even wider of the mark. The Paris and Orleans Railway has been operated on this basis since 1844, and up to 1882 more than $12,000,000 had been paid over *in profits* to employees. The intervention of the state, with a guarantee of at least ten per cent. of addition to the annual wage of each employee, has checked somewhat the operation of this principle; but its excellent effect, through many years, upon the conduct of the servants of the company is matter of history. "The employees," says M. Charles Robert, "mutually looked after each other. They had constantly in mind the thought of an eventual profit to be shared, of a possible loss to be avoided. Thus every one showed the greatest care in handling the passengers' luggage; and if an employee handled it

[1] *Profit Sharing in Industry*, p. 33.

unceremoniously, a comrade was not unfrequently heard saying to him, 'What are you about? You will shorten our dividend.' I have these details from a witness of authority."[1] Indeed, it is difficult to think of any other industry to which this principle could be applied more effectively than to this great railway traffic. To say that "the servants of a railway company, engine-drivers, guards, porters, and clerks contribute nothing to the success of the enterprise," is to exhibit an astonishing ignorance of affairs. On a recent visit to Chicago, I was met, on dismounting from the cab at the station of one of the great railways, by a porter, who relieved me at once of my hand-luggage, conducted my wife to the waiting-room, went with me to the office of the sleeping-car, and, while I was securing my berth, took my ticket and procured the check for my baggage, showed me the gate through which I should pass when my train was ready, and thus in the most polite and efficient manner attended to my comfort and put me at my ease; nor was there in his manner any suggestion of a fee. I am sure that if I ever have occasion to travel toward the Northwest again, I shall be strongly inclined to patronize that road. Whether this young man was interested in the profits of the road I do not know; but I do know that it is in the power of "guards" (we call them conductors), "porters, clerks," and other employees of a railway company to contribute very greatly to the comfort

[1] *Profit Sharing in Industry*, p. 84.

of passengers, to the popularity of the road, and thus to the success of the enterprise. And, so far as engine-drivers are concerned, it is not easy to exaggerate the extent to which the profits of the business depend on their coöperation. Not long ago, a practical railroad man, speaking without any thought of the question we are now considering, showed how easy it was for the engineer of a switch-engine, in making up freight trains on the sidings, to destroy property by the hundred dollars' worth, just through carelessness or ill-temper, by driving his cars together with a crash. The repair bills of most railroads are heavier in consequence of such recklessness or misconduct. And who can estimate the losses that are directly caused by the neglect or infidelity of railway employees! It may be said that the conscience of the employee should be a better safeguard against such injuries than his pecuniary interest, and I will not dispute that saying; but the problem is to bring his interest and his conscience more directly into line; to make his personal advantage more obviously identical with his duty to his employer. This is the problem which industrial partnership is trying to solve; it proposes to supplement the cash nexus of the wage system with the bond of mutual interest.

Three systems of participation in profits are practiced on the continent of Europe. One, the simplest, is like that which I have already described in the imaginary case. Another sets aside a share of the profits of the business annually for the employees, but, instead of paying it over to them at the end of the year, invests it at compound interest, and lets it accumulate until the employee has been for a certain number of years in the concern, or until he has reached a certain age. This system of deferred payment is the system of the insurance company of which I have spoken, and it has many advocates. But most of the participating houses combine these systems: part of the workman's share comes to him as a cash bonus at the end of the year; part of it is invested for his benefit. Let me mention a few typical instances.

M. Bord was a piano-maker in Paris, employing about four hundred men. In 1865 a strike in his establishment led to a treaty with his men, by which ten per cent. interest on his capital was to be drawn out of the profits every year by the employer, and the rest divided into two parts, one proportional to the amount already drawn as interest by the capitalist, the other proportional to the whole amount received as wages by the workmen. Each workman's share of this dividend was proportional also to the wages earned by him during the year. In 1866, the sum divided among the workmen was $3,235 ; in 1882, it was $26,025. The ratio of the bonus to the annual wages for these seventeen years is about sixteen per cent. The total of bonuses paid up to 1883 was $257,883. For only one year, that of the Franco-Prussian war, did the dividend fail. An addition to his wages, at the close of the year, of a bonus amounting to one sixth of all he had earned during the year would be regarded as a substantial gain by the average workingman; and this employer testifies that the arrangement is perfectly satisfactory to him in a pecuniary point of view, while "the effect of the system in attaching the workmen to the house, and its influence on their relation to their employer, are excellent."[1] The death of M. Bord in 1888 terminated this arrangement.

The Maison Chaix is a great printing, publishing, and bookselling house of Paris, employing nearly one thousand hands. Every year, M. Chaix, the head of the house, sets aside fifteen per cent. of the net profits for those of his workmen who have been in his employ three years or more; part of this is paid over to them in cash, and part put into a savings account on which interest is paid. The total amount allotted to them in ten years was about $130,000, of which $31,000 was paid over in cash bonuses. Annual meetings of the employees are held, at which the employer explains the state of the business to them, and makes known the amount of their dividends. Reports of some of these admirable speeches are found in Mr. Taylor's book. In his address to his people delivered in 1879, M. Chaix says: "In what concerns the execution of work in the workshops and the offices, I find around me such an amount of willing zeal that I give the main credit for this excellent state of things to profit sharing, and congratulate myself

[1] *Profit Sharing in Industry*, p. 31.

more and more on having set that principle working in this house."[1] This is a business man, an employer, talking to his employees. Some other ideas besides competition and supply and demand seem to have got possession of his mind.

MM. Billon et Isaac, manufacturers of music-boxes at Geneva, work on a different plan. They deduct from the profits of the year interest on capital and payments to the reserve fund, and then they divide the remainder into two equal parts, one of which goes to the owners, and the other to the laborers. But the laborers' share is also divided into two equal parts, one of which is paid to them in cash, and the other is invested in twenty-dollar shares of the company, which make them owners, entitle them to vote at the general meetings, and bring them annual interest. This has been in operation more than twenty years, in every one of which, except the year of the Russo-Turkish war, there has been a dividend, which has averaged, for the whole time, about fifteen per cent. of the annual wages. A letter from one of the workmen contains these words: "The undersigned has been working for the last eight years in this factory; . . . and he can testify that participation in profits has entirely altered the mode of life and habits of the workmen. Formerly, no one thought save of himself and of his individual interests; quarrels about work were nothing out of the common way. Now, on the contrary, all consider themselves as

[1] *Profit Sharing in Industry*, p. 55.

members of one and the same family, and the good of the establishment has become the object of every one's solicitude, because our own personal interest is bound up with it. It is with pleasure that one remarks how each man strives to fill up his time with conscientious effort, to effect the utmost possible saving in the materials, to collect carefully the fallen chips of metal; and how, if one or other now is guilty of some negligence, a joking remark from his neighbor suffices to bring him to order again." Seventy of the employees of this establishment in 1871 signed a letter of which this is a part: "The workman, having the same interests as his employers, and perceiving that he is no longer treated like a machine, works with energy and courage; our hearts are warmed and cheered by contact with those of our employers who are always ready to set us a good example."[1] The employer is equally enthusiastic. In 1880, he writes thus: "After ten years of experience, we congratulate ourselves more and more on having adopted this principle. Its application has to such a degree become ingrained into our modes of doing business that we should not know how to get on without it. The management of an undertaking appears to us no longer possible without this element of justice, harmony, and peace."[2]

There is one story more stirring by far than any I have told. It is the story of the Maison Leclaire, a great house-painting business established in Paris,

[1] *Profit Sharing in Industry*, p. 38. [2] *Ibid.*

in 1842, on the participatory basis, by Edme-Jean Leclaire, one of the noblest of modern philanthropists. No profuse and careless almsgiver was this keen-witted Frenchman: he was a prosperous business man; he left a snug little fortune of $240,000. But his ruling motive was his desire to improve the condition of the men in his employ. Ponder these words of his, written when death was near, and when, as he said, he felt sincerity to be more than ever a duty:—

"I believe in the God who has written in our hearts the law of duty, the law of progress, the law of the sacrifice of one's self for others. I submit myself to his will; I bow before the mysteries of his power and of our destiny. I am the humble disciple of Him who has told us to do to others what we would have others do to us, and to love our neighbors as ourselves: it is in this sense that I desire to remain a Christian until my last breath."[1]

In this spirit he was pondering the case of his workmen in 1835, when an old philosopher named Fregier, listening to his queries, answered that he saw no way to get rid of the antagonism between workman and master *except by the participation of the workman in the profits* of the master. That seed fell into good soil; out of it sprang the Maison Leclaire, and the broadening harvest of participatory industries which are filling France with peace and plenty. This great house, whose work has been going on prosperously in the hands of

[1] *Profit Sharing in Industry*, p. 25.

Leclaire's successors since his death which occurred in 1872, employs more than a thousand men, transacts a business of more than $600,000 a year, and divides as bonus about $45,000 a year, which adds about one fifth to the wages of the men. The sum paid out of profits to the workmen, in addition to their wages, from 1842 to 1882, amounted to $665,225.

In Mr. Gilman's list of 135 profit sharing firms now in successful operation only eight English firms are included. A later list, compiled in 1892, names 75 firms in Great Britain now working on this basis. This shows a very rapid extension of the system in England within the last five years.

In our own country this participatory method has been in operation for many years with brilliant success in one industry, the fisheries of Massachusetts. I have also statistics of thirty or forty manufacturing and mercantile establishments in this country which have adopted some form of participation. Several of them are among our most enterprising and successful concerns, such as the Pillsbury Mills, in Minneapolis; N. O. Nelson & Co., of St. Louis; the Bucyrus Foundry Co., in Ohio; the Proctor and Gamble Co., in Cincinnati, Rogers, Peet & Co. and the Century Company, in New York; the Rumford Chemical Works, in East Providence, R. I.; H. O. Houghton & Co., of the Riverside Press, Cambridge, Mass.; the Springfield Foundry Co., of Springfield, Mass.; the Ara Cushman Co., of Auburn, Maine; the Yale and

Towne Manufacturing Co., of Stamford, Conn.; Alfred Dolge & Co., of Dolgeville, N. Y.; Rand, McNally & Co., of Chicago; John Wanamaker & Co. and the Public Ledger Co., of Philadelphia; the Toledo, Ann Arbor and Michigan Railway. Two other very important railways — the "Big Four" system and the Cairo "Short Line" — have the matter under consideration. The workman's share in the profits is in some of these concerns quite small; in others it is considerable. Some of the firms are able to add only three or four per cent. a year to the amount of their pay-roll; others have been able to increase the aggregate annual wage of their men by ten per cent., or even larger amounts. Mr. George W. Childs adds about ten per cent. to the wages of his printers; Mr. Wanamaker distributes, according to a system of his own, bonuses and extra payments, amounting in 1888 to about $100,000; Proctor & Gamble have added from 9.33 per cent. to 13.47 per cent. to the wages of their men; and the Pillsburys have been able, in some years, to increase the stipend of their trusted men by as much as $400 to each one. Even the smaller percentages amount to quite as much, in most cases, as the net gains of strikes that are regarded as successful. If a company of workmen strike for ten per cent. increase of wages, and gain their point, the expense of the strike, in most cases, consumes more than half of the gain for a year to come. Five per cent. would, therefore, be the entire net gain. Is not a peaceful arrangement with the employer, by which even so small an increase as five per cent. of the annual wage is secured, greatly to be preferred to a strike which results in a nominal increase of ten per cent.? It is only within the past four or five years that the system of profit sharing has been adopted to any extent in the United States. The tardiness of our people in making this experiment is not easily accounted for; it would seem that the first successes of this democratic idea should have been won upon our own soil. The recent labor troubles have opened the eyes of a great many persons to the need of discovering a better basis for industrial society, and quite a number of establishments have recently admitted the workmen to a limited partnership. We shall soon be able, therefore, to study at shorter range the operations of this method.

The facts which I have already presented are sufficient, however, to convince any reasonable man that this system is practicable. It rests on no man's conjectures; it stands on a solid basis of achievement. A committee of the French Parliament, reporting on this system in 1882, bore this testimony: "This application of a great principle has already passed beyond the region of mere theory, and has received in large measure the sanction of experience. . . . Participation, under all the varied forms which it has assumed, can point to brilliant attained results." [1]

The excellent report of the Massachusetts Bu-

[1] *Profit Sharing in Industry*, p. 48.

reau of Statistics presents these among other cardinal principles of industrial partnership: —

"Participation by workmen in profits, in addition to wages, is a true harmonizer of the interests of capital and labor. It does, in fact, identify the interest of the employed with the interest of the employer. It converts the industrial association of employer and employee into a moral organism, in which all the various talents, services, and desires of the component individuals are fused into a community of purpose and endeavor.

"The dividend to labor is not, usually, an increase of pay, services remaining the same, but a form of extra pay for extra services and an inducement calling them out.

"The extra services called out, and the manner of calling them out, constitute an invaluable educational discipline. They develop the whole group of industrial virtues, diligence, fidelity, care-taking, economy, continuity of effort, willingness to learn, and the spirit of coöperation."[1]

It is not the workingmen alone who will be the gainers by this reorganization of labor. To the employers the advantage will be quite as substantial. The peace thus won will be the handmaid of plenty. War is a costly business; the saving of this increasing cost will be an enormous gain. And the removal of the causes of anxiety and irritation is also a result worth some expenditure. To one who is, by virtue of his calling, an ex-

[1] *Report for* 1886, p. 231.

tremely "unpractical" man, it sometimes seems that if he were a "practical" man he would not try to run a complicated piece of machinery without adequate lubrication. The lubricating oil may be somewhat expensive, but is it not less expensive than frequent stoppages from hot journals, and the occasional burning down of your building from the same frictional inflammation? I have a little book on this subject, in which it is shown that out of 575 fires in mills 37 per cent. were caused by friction and bad lubrication. Prudent mechanicians are not unwilling to incur the trouble and expense of adequate lubrication. And it seems to me that the social side of the machinery needs lubrication as well as the physical side. The very complicated mechanism of organized labor must be frequently and carefully oiled. The bearings will get hot, there will be frequent and costly stoppages and casualties, if care is not taken to avoid friction. What is wanted is the sweet oil of kindness, consideration, generosity, sympathy, on the part of the employer. Doubtless it costs something to keep the machinery properly lubricated; it costs time and thought and patience, and some money; but would it not pay?

Another important advantage to the employer is the enforced conservatism in the conduct of his business which the system demands. The reserve fund is an essential feature of this plan; and the reserve fund will prove the salvation of the business in many a period of stringency.

But best of all the fruits of this system will be the effect upon the character of the employer. The honest attempt to put this scheme into operation will prove an "invaluable educational discipline" to him. In him, also, it will develop a group of virtues, not identical with those named above which it tends to bring forth in the character of the laborer, but virtues of great preciousness, and virtues which unmodified competition does not cherish. Sympathy, consideration, the sense of stewardship, the responsibility of power, the chivalrous regard for those whom we are called to shelter and to serve, — all these fine qualities must surely be nourished in the heart of the employer who earnestly endeavors to put his business on a participatory basis. He will unlearn any lordly or dictatorial ways that he may have fallen into; he will cease to think of the business as exclusively his concern, and will begin to regard it as the joint enterprise of the men who furnish the capital and the men who do the work; he will often, in his hours of thought, gather his helpers about him, and speak to them, not audibly with the lips, yet reverently in the heart, those words of a greater Master: "Henceforth I call you not servants; I call you friends."

For it is only when this spirit, or some measure of it, finds a place in the heart of the employer that this method of industry can be introduced with assurance of success. Mr. Taylor is right when he says that this is no "self-acting panacea," and that it can never be worked by men who care for nothing but money. No man whose only thought of his employees is how to get out of them the most work for the least wages will ever succeed with this method. Such a man will never succeed by any method in getting anything but the ill-will of his employees. The best fruits of participation, says Mr. Taylor, "can be reached only by men who feel that life does not consist in abundance of material possessions, and who regard stewardship as nobler than ownership." It is only in the spirit of Leclaire that the system of which he was the illustrious protagonist can be made to yield its largest benefits.

Industrial partnership is simply the attempt to reorganize labor with some regard to the Christian law; its superiority to the unmodified wage system consists in the fact that it gives to Christian motives larger room and freer play.

It seems to me that we have come, in the evolution of our industrial system, to the stage at which the general introduction of participation is expedient and imperative. Such a concession as it requires capital cannot too speedily make; such a recognition of the dignity of labor as it involves the employing classes cannot too frankly utter. We shall not stop with this; we shall go farther; how much farther it is impossible to tell; but it will be wiser, I think, for the laboring classes not to be in haste, and it will be wiser for the employing classes not to refuse the readjustments which will allay the present discontent. "A question arises here," wrote Carlyle almost fifty years ago, "whether in some ulterior, perhaps some not far distant stage of this 'Chivalry of Labour' your master-worker may not find it possible and needful to grant his workers permanent *interest* in his enterprise and theirs. So that it becomes, in practical result, what in essential fact and justice it ever is, a joint enterprise; all men, from the chief master down to the lowest overseer and operative, economically as well as loyally concerned for it." Carlyle answered his own question rather dubiously. No man could answer it confidently whose detestation of democracy was as cordial as his. But to some of us it seems that the very terms in which his question is proposed contain the answer. If "in essential fact and justice" every industrial enterprise "ever is a joint enterprise," then it is certain in due season to become so. The essential fact and justice are going to get themselves recognized and established in this world by and by. And the business of every Christian is to discern the essential fact and justice, to make his own conduct conform to it, and to strive to get it recognized and established here in the world as speedily as possible. If we can only get these essential principles of Christianity rooted in the convictions of all classes, we may safely leave them to work out their own results. But it may be helpful to deduce a few inferential maxims of practical application.

Employers must not forget that the large system of industry involves the *association of men* as capitalists and laborers — *social organization*, in fact; and all forms of social organization call for a large infusion of the altruistic element. Society cannot be built on the basis of commercial contract. You who gather men together for these great industries have constant need to remember these words of Carlyle: "Love of men cannot be bought by cash-payment; and without love men cannot endure to be together." Somehow you must manage to supply that cement to the industrial society which you have organized.

The old maxim *noblesse oblige* is binding upon the captains of industry. Because they have the superior intelligence and the natural gifts of leadership they must take the initiative in all plans for the reorganization of industry. Hear Carlyle again: "The main substance of this immense problem of Organizing Labor, and first of all of managing the working classes, will, it is very clear, have to be solved by those who stand practically in the middle of it; by those who themselves work and preside over work."

In the working out of these plans it will be necessary for employers to use great patience, to take their workmen into their confidence, and to explain very fully the nature of the partnership which they are forming. Read the story of Jean Godin and his *Familistère* at Guise, and learn how this great-hearted employer met his workmen night after night for weeks, laying before them his plans for their welfare, discussing all the details, allaying their suspicions, and finally winning their consent to become partners with him in the great industry of which they will soon be the sole proprietors. The failure of these industrial partnerships has often been due to the neglect of the employers to come to a good understanding with their workmen. The whole business has been managed at arm's length; the concession was rather surlily offered at the beginning, never clearly explained, and rather suspiciously accepted; there was fear on both sides of bad faith and overreaching. No partnership will thrive in such an atmosphere. But those who approach the problem in the spirit and temper of Jean Godin will generally find that the solution is not impossible.

The greatest opportunities of this generation, the opportunities of Christian leadership, of Christian statesmanship, are offered to the employers of labor. They are called to moralize the industrial realm whose ruling law has hitherto been pagan. They are called to lead in that peaceful reconstruction of our industries by which labor and capital shall be identified in interest and feeling, and peace shall be established among men. I believe that some of them have heard the call, and are rising to their opportunity. Knightlier work can no man do than that which awaits them. May God fill them with wisdom and courage and patience and love!

There are one or two truths which workingmen also will do well to bear in mind.

It must not be supposed that by any arrangements which men can make, industrial, economic, or political, the eternal laws can be circumvented. Men are not all alike. They differ vastly in endowment. The services that some men render to society are far greater than those rendered by others. Their reward ought to be and will be proportionately greater. It is a great service that any man renders to society who organizes and successfully manages a great industry. It is a great service to the men employed; probably not one in five of them, working as his own master, could secure as large a reward for his labor as he receives under the direction of this master. It is a great service to the community at large to have the aggregate product of industry enlarged and cheapened. "The function of the man of business," says one of the later economists, "is essentially that of coördinating the factors and processes of the economic world — labor, capital, invention, and superintendence in the factory, supply and demand in the market. Throughout organic nature, and no less in human society, the coördinating function is useful and costly compared with the mere expenditure of energy in direct and simple ways." It is useful and it is costly. Great services deserve great rewards. That is one of the eternal laws. Any socialistic scheme that ignores it will come to grief. Coöperation is industrial democracy, but democracy is not communism; it implies leadership; it argues that when factitious distinctions are swept away the natural leaders will come to the front. Shake apples in a basket and the biggest ones will rise to the top. That is the law of nature, and it will get itself enforced. "All flesh is not the same flesh," and all brains are not of the same size. And brains will tell. In all your thoughts about the new régime of industry, keep this in mind.

Neither must it be imagined that any arrangement will ever be effected that will cancel the natural penalties of ignorance and indolence and improvidence. A large share of the misfortunes of the working classes arise from these sources. I know, for I have been working with them and for them for thirty years. Whatever the form of the industrial organization, it will always be true that for many workingmen reform must begin at home, in improved habits of industry, thrift, and sobriety.

"Coöperation," as we have seen, "awaits the advent of the coöperative man." He is coming, but his coming can be hastened by cultivating a spirit of candor, moderation, and sweet reasonableness. Workingmen who would like to enter into partnership with their employer would do well to let him see that their temper is such as to promise pleasant and profitable relations.

And now a final word that applies with equal force to employers and employed. Whether your place is at the lathe or in the counting-room, you are bound to consider, not your individual interest alone, nor merely that of the corporation whose agent you are, nor merely that of the trades-union to which you belong, but also and always the interest of the whole community. "No man liveth unto himself!" How much truer that is to-day than when it was written! "Modern production is not an individualistic process, it is the act of society as a whole," says a recent writer. We are all bound together in interest and welfare; whether we will or no, the law of our civilization is, "Each for all and all for each." Every industrial war injures the whole commonwealth. We must learn to think of these inevitable and far-reaching effects of our conduct. It will not do for us to get into the habit of saying, "This business is mine, and I propose to manage it to suit myself;" or to fall into the way of thinking that the little group of workers to which we belong contains the only people whose welfare is to be considered. We are members one of another, and we must think and act for the interest of all. That is the Christian way of thinking and acting, and when we all learn that way, we shall have reached the end of our centuries of strife, and have come to the beginning of the thousand years of peace.

IX.

SCIENTIFIC SOCIALISM.

WE have been studying certain proposed modifications of the present industrial order, by which it is hoped that a greater identity of interest between employer and employed might be secured. But there are many in these days who have no hope that the present industrial order can be improved, and who are of the opinion that the only thing feasible is to abolish it altogether.

Of these there are several classes, which must be carefully distinguished. Socialists, Communists, and Anarchists or Nihilists agree in their condemnation of the present system of industry, but are by no means at one in their theories of what should take its place.

Communism is mainly a scheme for the better distribution of wealth; it cares less about how it is produced and fixes its attention on getting it evenly divided. Socialism is chiefly concerned about the production of wealth, and although it aims at lessening the inequalities which now exist, it does not usually insist on its being equally divided. Under Communism there is no private property; under Socialism there might be private property, but could be no private enterprise. The industries of the land would be regulated, under Socialism, by the state; every farm, every factory, every railroad, every mine, would be managed by the government. The proposition of Socialism is to extend the power of the state over all the productive and distributive industries of the nation; so that every man who works shall work for the state, and receive as his stipend, not money, for money under that régime would be impossible, but labor-checks entitling him to obtain in the government store houses a certain amount of goods. All these goods, produced by labor, would be valued by the amount of labor expended in producing them; therefore each man would directly exchange his labor for the products of other men's labor, and the exchange would be made through the medium of the state. Such, in the barest outline, is the socialistic scheme. It is evident that it could not be put into operation without a sweeping political revolution. Communism may exist under any form of government; it does exist under our government; the Shakers, the Icarians, the Zoarites, are all Communists. But Socialism could not come into full sway without a more tremendous social upheaval than ever yet took place in any civilized society.

It may also be well to distinguish between Socialism and what is known as Nihilism or Anarchism. The Anarchist denounces all government; he wants to destroy the existing social and political order, root and branch, and leave every man free to do that which is right in his own eyes. He imagines that some sort of order would spring out of this chaos, but he neither knows nor cares what it would be. He is, therefore, theoretically at exactly the opposite end of the scale from the Socialist. The Socialist wants the government to do everything; the Anarchist wants the government to do nothing. Yet, wide apart as these two are in their theories, we sometimes find them acting together. Extremes meet. The Socialist is willing that the Anarchist should destroy the existing order, so that he may build his own on its ruins. But just as soon as the present order was destroyed, the bitterest foe that the Socialist would have to fight would be the Anarchist.

Anarchists are few, and Communists are few, but Socialists are many. "Socialism," says Professor Walker, "was never more full of lusty vigor, more rich in the promise of things to come than now." The movement of thought in this direction has been very rapid during the last ten years. Nor is this scheme, which seems so audacious, so revolutionary, wholly the product of cranks and criminals; let no man imagine it. The philosophers of Socialism are men of deep insight and strong logic. Rodbertus, Marx, Lassalle, are thinkers and statesmen who need not stoop in the presence of the strong men of our time. And it cannot be denied that the movement of the leaders of opinion, of independent students of social science, has been for twenty years in the direction of Socialism. The word, indeed, has come to be a kind of cudgel with which disputants in the field of political science are wont to assail one another. Socialism, as we have seen, signifies the extension of the sphere of the state over the greater part of our industrial life. The strict disciple of *laissez faire* regards every assumption by the state of power outside of its police function as a species of Socialism. Whenever the state undertakes to do anything in the way of promoting the general welfare, it is following, say these philosophers, a socialistic tendency. With this definition most of us are Socialists. Prince Bismarck avows himself a Socialist and with some reason; in his insurance and pension schemes he has used the power of the state in a vigorous fashion to promote the welfare of the working classes. The Tory aristocrats of England, like Lord Shaftesbury, who secured the enactment of the factory legislation were, as Arnold Toynbee proves, a kind of Socialists. Mr. Herbert Spencer is not exactly a Socialist; he is rather more of an Anarchist, for he thinks that government is essentially and universally an evil; yet he denounces private ownership in land in words which, as Mr. Sidgwick says, make Henry George sound like a plagiarist. He demands that the government take possession of the land and hold it for the benefit of the whole people. So far he goes with the Socialists. In the main, however, he is the keen and relentless opponent of everything that savors of Socialism. Mr. Spencer is, indeed, the leader of a most formidable revolt against socialistic tendencies. A recent volume of essays entitled "A Plea for Liberty," to which Mr. Spencer contributes the introductory essay, is perhaps the strongest philosophical attack which has lately been made upon the main positions of the Socialists.

We find, therefore, two pronounced schools of thought rapidly developing into parties, and the air is full of their fierce debate. After a little we shall be able, I trust, to see what hot partisans on either side are apt to forget, that social progress is always the resultant of two steadily acting tendencies, — the tendency to the perfection of the individual, and the tendency to the more perfect and harmonious coöperation of individuals; and that healthy progress is maintained only when both these tendencies are active and positive. Neither of these ends can be attained without the other. The individual cannot be perfected without a large and intelligent and hearty coöperation with the society in which he lives; and society cannot be perfected without the development of the manhood of the individuals who compose it. Both these ends must be steadily held in view in all wise social construction. Neither must take precedence of the other; the one is just as important as the other. They have the same relation to the progress of the race that the two wings of the bird sustain to its motion through the air. If either wing is broken or lamed, there is no such thing as flight; there may be much fluttering, but there is no escape from the earth, no progress through the air. And as a bird cannot fly without two wings, so the community cannot rise and advance without the integrity of the individual on the one hand, and the thorough identification of the individual with the life of his fellows on the other.

That perverse habit of looking on one side of a question, which is the source of many of our social troubles, is strikingly illustrated in the way in which each of these complementary truths has gathered a party, which takes its formula for a watchword, and advocates it, as inconsistent with and hostile to the other. One who listens to these factions as they contend with each other wonders whether we may not some time have two parties, one of which shall maintain that hooks alone are useful, and that eyes are nugatory; while the other will insist that hooks are superfluous, and that there is no utility in anything but eyes; or whether there may not arise two schools of physiologists, one of which shall assert that the human body is of no importance; that all that is of value is the separate parts and organs, — the head and the feet and the hands, the heart and the liver and the lungs, and so forth; while the other school maintains that it is the body alone that is of consequence, and that the recognition of and the care for these separate parts and organs is unscientific and absurd. When in the evolution of intellectual freaks these controversies shall arise, those who witness them will be able to show that they are not exceptional monstrosities of one-sided theorizing; that precisely the same kind of dispute was going on in the last part of the nineteenth century between the Individualists and the Socialists.

For the first three quarters of this century the prevailing social philosophy was individualistic; during the last quarter, thus far, the Socialists have had their innings, and they have made the most of it; the tendency, even among the scholars, to a socialistic interpretation of society has been very strong. With much of what the Socialists are saying, every philanthropist must be in closest accord. The criticisms which they have uttered upon the cruel and destructive tendencies of our industrial system have been timely and in great part true. That competition, when wholly unrestrained, must tend to make the rich richer and the poor poorer; that the growth of a plutocracy at one end of the social scale and of a proletariat at the other are the natural and inevitable result of *laissez faire*, — all this is evident to-day, and the Socialists have helped to keep it before our thought. The growing chasm between employer and employee; the feverish condition of the industrial world; the increasing frequency of depressions in trade, every one of which pushes a crowd of poor laborers into actual pauperism, — all these ominous signs, to which the Socialists keep pointing us, are evidence that something is wrong with the industrial machinery. So, at any rate, it looks to me. Yet I find Mr. Spencer and his friends denying that any such conditions exist. The working people, they say, are in far better case now than they ever were before. "Any one," says Mr. Spencer, "who can look back sixty years, when the amount of pauperism was far greater than now and beggars abundant, is struck by the comparative size and finish of the new houses occupied by operatives, by the better dress of workmen who wear broadcloth on Sundays, and of servant girls who vie with their mistresses, — by the higher standard of living which leads to a great demand for the best qualities of food by working people; all results of the double change to higher wages and cheaper commodities and a distribution of taxes which has relieved the lower classes at the expense of the higher classes."[1] And one of Mr. Spencer's associates, in the volume from which this is quoted, declares that the "socialist declamation" with respect to the growing misery of the working classes "is only true, if true at all, of the lowest residuum, and [that] that residuum is no more than a fringe on the border of society in any country where the capitalist is free."[2] Here is a pretty serious question of fact. What Mr. Spencer says of the general elevation of the standard of living among the working classes is substantially true. There have been gains and great gains in the con-

[1] *A Plea for Liberty*, p. 3. [2] *Ibid.* p. 34.

dition of the mass of wage-workers. But there are still two important questions not quite satisfactorily answered. First, Have these gains been proportionate to the increase of the aggregate wealth of the community? Second, Is it true that what Professor Graham calls the "social residuum," and what General Booth calls "the submerged tenth," is growing faster than the population? It is impossible in this place adequately to discuss these questions. But I will venture to quote, as throwing light upon them, the words of Mr. Robert Giffen, the English statistician, whose calculations and conclusions with respect to the existing order have always been extremely optimistic. In an essay on "The Gross and Net Gain of Rising Wages," Mr. Giffen professes his faith that we shall see in the immediate future "a continuous improvement, on the average, of the human being who really belongs to the new society." But he makes this important concession: —

"The one doubtful sign, it appears to me, as regards the future, is pointed at by the qualification implied in the words, *the human being who really belongs to the new society*. It may probably happen that there will be an increase, or at least non-diminution of what may be called the social wreckage. A class may continue to exist and even increase in the midst of our civilization, probably not a large class in proportion, but still a considerable class, who are out of the improvement altogether, who are capable of nothing but the rudest labor, and who have neither the moral nor the mental faculties fitted for the strain of the work of modern society. On the other side, as already hinted, the existence of what may be called a barbarian class among the capitalist classes, living in idle luxury and not bearing the burden of society in any way, seems also a danger." [1]

There is, then, a serious "social wreckage" resulting from the swift relentless movement of modern society; it may be increasing, in spite of the enormous aggregate gains of material wealth and comfort. And one of the distinct purposes of Socialism, as I understand it, is to prevent this social wreckage. To this proposition Mr. Spencer and his school make answer, first, by denying that there is any such social wreckage, or at any rate that the amount of it is increasing; and in this answer I am persuaded that they are quite too optimistic. But, in the second place, they say to the Socialists, "Even admitting the growth of the social residuum, your way of trying to check its growth would only increase its growth; while your method of preventing social wreckage would result in stopping progress altogether." And in this answer I think that they are partly right. But then, if they are pressed with the assertion that this increase of the social residuum is a terrible fact, and with the demand to know what they propose to do about it, they answer, for substance, "We will do what we can, by alms, to relieve this

[1] *The Contemporary Review*, December, 1889.

distress; but we do not disguise from ourselves the fact that we cannot do much; the only solution is in the application of the law of the survival of the fittest; the people who have not the strength to catch hold of this swiftly moving industrial train and hold on may as well be dropped; if they perish by the way, even in increasing numbers, they are only fulfilling the evolutionary law; thus society sloughs off its waste material, and relieves itself of its incumbrances and goes forward the more swiftly in the path of progress."

This is, I think, a consistent and logical answer. It is the legitimate outcome of the doctrine of *laissez faire*. It is the natural fruit of Cain's philosophy, "Am I my brother's keeper?" It is not, however, the Christian way of looking at the social problem. It is as far from Christianity, its sentiments, and its principles of action, as the east is from the west. The effect which the adoption of this method would have upon society may be easily conjectured. It might, very likely, add temporarily to its material wealth. The extermination of the weak and the dependent should result in a great increase of productive energy. But the simultaneous paralysis or atrophy of the instincts of compassion, of the sentiments of kindness and charity, would bring about a state of society in which even these strenuous individualists would, I think, soon find themselves uncomfortable. It is evident that social gains of this description might be purchased at too great a cost. For we must not forget that we are not only wealth-producing and wealth-consuming creatures, that we are also human beings, and that with all our gettings we must not lose our humanity. It is largely because these keen individualists seem to place too little emphasis upon this cardinal fact that we are disinclined to follow them. Even among the disciples of this school there are some who begin to shrink from the unsocialism to which its teachings lead. Professor Sidgwick is, perhaps, the ablest living expositor of the Ricardian economy, and he is frank enough to admit its immoral tendencies. "For instance," he says, "we should consider it extortionate in a boatman who happened to be the only man able to save valuable works of art from being lost in a river to demand for his services a reward manifestly beyond their normal price — that is, beyond the price which, under ordinary circumstances, competition would determine at that time and place. Still, it is by no means clear that such extortion is 'contrary to the principles of Political Economy,' as ordinarily understood. Economists assume in their scientific discussions — frequently with more or less approval of the conduct assumed — that every enlightened person will try to sell his commodity in the dearest market; and the dearest market is, *ceteris paribus*, wherever the need for such commodity is greatest." And then this eminent economist proceeds, in sober words to which I beg to call your very careful attention: "A consideration of facts like these leads us naturally to the widest and deepest question that the subject . . . suggests, whether, namely, the whole individualistic organization of industry, whatever its material advantages may be, is not open to condemnation as radically demoralizing. Not a few enthusiastic persons have been led to this conclusion, partly from the difficulty of demonstrating the general harmony of private and common interest . . . partly from an aversion *to the anti-social temper and attitude of mind, produced by the continual struggle of competition*, even when it is admittedly advantageous to production. Such moral aversion is certainly an important, though not the most powerful, element in the impulses that lead thoughtful people to embrace some form of Socialism. And many who are not Socialists, regarding the stimulus and direction of energy given by the existing individualistic system as quite indispensable to human society as at present constituted, yet feel the moral need of some means of developing in the members of a modern industrial community a fuller consciousness of their industrial work as a social function, only rightly performed when done with a cordial regard to the welfare of the whole society, or at least of that part of it to which the work is immediately useful."[1]

Here, now, is a fact on which Mr. Giffen's figures and Mr. Atkinson's graphic tables throw no light whatever, and yet it is by far the deepest and most important fact of the whole discussion. No

[1] *Principles of Political Economy*, pp. 585–590.

matter what the material gains of the present age may be, if the moral outcome of the competitive system is what Mr. Sidgwick says it is ; if the tendency of all our schooling in trade and business is to make us heartless and unscrupulous and careless of the welfare of our fellow-men, — to breed a race of strong, fierce, unmoral materialists, whose gains are gotten by despoiling their fellows, — then the present system is doomed ; and the more rapid its growth has been, the speedier and the more disastrous will be its downfall. When there is no consciousness in the members of the industrial community that their work is a social function, only "rightly performed when done with a cordial regard to the welfare of the whole society ;" when, instead of this, they adopt the maxim of individualism, so succinctly expressed by Professor Sumner, that "the supreme result of modern society is to guarantee to every man the use of all his powers exclusively for his own benefit," then confusion and strife and every evil work must certainly increase and abound. It is this *Unsocialism*, fierce and cruel, as Professor Sidgwick says, that has given rise to Socialism. The doctrines of Winkelblech and Rodbertus, of Robert Owen and Lassalle, are in large part the reaction of a scourged and outraged humanity against the greed and rapacity of the individualistic régime.

Partly, then, because of the social wreckage which, under the present system of industry, seems to be increasing, and partly because of the unsocial tempers which are generated by it, many of us are strongly inclined to listen to the Socialists when they come preaching a new dispensation. And it is a very engaging gospel which we hear from their lips. Poverty is to be abolished; there is to be work for all and all are to be required to work, and all will earn by their work an ample livelihood; the feud of rich and poor will come to an end; peace and plenty will fill the earth. And there shall be no more curse; the egoistic impulse will have spent its force; good-will will rule instead of greed: —

> "The crown of the getter shall fall to the donor,
> And last shall be first while first shall be last,
> And to love best shall still be to reign unsurpassed."

This is what we are waiting for; if the Socialists can assure us of it, they shall have our suffrages. But we have a right to demand clear evidence of their power when thus they offer us the kingdoms of this world and their glory. Especially when they speak in the name of science are we entitled to subject their schemes to a rigid scrutiny. And this is the claim of the recent Socialism. It professes to give us a reasoned philosophy of society; it undertakes to demonstrate that its programme is in harmony with the natural laws of the social order.

It is precisely here that our faith meets its first and severest shock. Whatever else modern Socialism may be, it is not scientific. Its reasonings about the facts of the social order are not sound reasonings. Its account of what is taking place in the industrial world is not a true account. What is the scientific basis of modern Socialism? Let Professor Graham make answer: "The theory of value, in the hands of Karl Marx, is in fact almost the whole of Socialism. According to Dr. Schaeffle, the most candid as well as the keenest critic of Socialism, the theory is in the strictest sense the basis of Socialism." I have referred, in a former chapter, to the theory of Marx, and have endeavored to show its unsoundness. This theory is that labor is the source of all value; that all the wealth in the world is due to labor. There is no time here to deal with this fundamental fallacy, but any one who will carefully study the question in the light of all the recent economic investigation will very speedily find out that the theory is groundless. I may not assume to be an authority in economics, but I will offer three or four witnesses, all of whom are men who strongly sympathize with the purposes of the Socialists.

The first shall be Professor Smart, of Glasgow: "Taking its stand on one part of the Ricardian theory of value, and ignoring the other, [Socialism] writes out its economic system from the fundamental proposition that labor is the sole source of value. . . . The indefensible point of this is, of course, its account of value. . . . The 'value' of economic science must be what men call and think and will recognize as value, and not what it would suit the theorist to call value. . . . Value is not the easy thing it is in socialist theory. Its origin and measure are not decided by the consideration that labor rightly applied can produce valuable things. Labor expended is merely the symptom that value is expected, not its cause. What we can say is that labor is economically employed when making valuable things. What we must deny is that any amount or kind of human labor will give value to what the world, as we know it, does not wish and will not have."[1]

The second witness is Professor Naquet, of Paris: "The first objection that may be raised against the conclusions of Karl Marx rests on his theory of value, which is totally unscientific. According to Karl Marx, an object is strictly worth what it has cost to produce, and is worth nothing more. This conception is absolutely erroneous. The cost of production, if it enters as an element in the fixing of value, does so only in a subsidiary manner, simply as a matter of consequence, and leaves the chief and fundamental place to utility."[2]

And Professor Naquet goes on to show how objects on which no labor has been expended possess great value, and how other objects on which great labor has been expended possess no value at all.

My third witness shall be Emile de Laveleye, the eminent Belgian economist: "The fundamental error of Marx lies in the idea he conceives of value,

[1] *Annals of the American Academy*, vol. iii. pp. 4, 5.
[2] *Collectivism*, p. 10.

which, according to him, is always in proportion to labor. . . . Beyond question labor is an essential element of value, but whenever society, that is to say, natural or social monopoly, intervenes — and when does it not? — labor is not the sole element. . . . In fine, we may say that the mighty and pretentious attempt of Marx to overturn the foundations of existing society, while relying on the very principles of Political Economy, has failed because he has only strung together a number of abstract formulas, without ever going to the root of things." [1]

My fourth witness shall be Professor Graham, of Dublin, who, after a long and careful analysis of the doctrine in question, concludes: "Thus, then, the Marxian theory of value and theoretical basis of Socialism is vicious as a theory and inapplicable in practice." [2]

It is hardly necessary to multiply authorities. It is sufficient to say that the great majority of modern economists — those who are most strongly inclined to find some better way of organizing society than the present way — are agreed that the account which Marx has given of the present industrial order is not a true account. The fundamental trouble with Scientific Socialism is that it is unscientific, that it does not clearly understand and explain existing facts. And when we find that a man does not understand the present, we are not strongly inclined to take his word about

[1] *Socialism of To-Day*, pp. 34–39.
[2] *Socialism New and Old*, p. 212.

the future. If the things that are going on before his eyes are not clear to him, how can we be sure that the untried scheme which he commends to us will work in the way he expects it to work? Such is the fundamental difficulty which we encounter when we begin to examine critically the theories of the Socialists. And as we pursue our studies the difficulties multiply. Let us mention a few of them.

The radical difficulty with Socialism in a scientific point of view lies in the fact that it underrates the functions of mind in production. When Socialists say that all value is the product of labor, they generally mean muscular labor, or else they insist that mental labor shall be reduced to the terms of muscular labor. Rodbertus says that labor is the only productive agent and the only source of value, and although he includes under this term intellectual as well as physical labor, he goes on to say that physical labor is *immediately* productive, and should therefore receive a share in *direct* distribution, while intellectual labor is *mediately* productive, and is entitled to share in *derivative* distribution. Now all labor is partly physical and partly intellectual. The difference between skilled and unskilled labor is that the one calls into action more intellect than the other. But according to this definition the more skill there is in labor, the less "immediately" productive it is and the less "directly" it should share in the gains of industry. According to this theory, also, the work of the master builder who organizes and directs the labor of a hundred men is less immediately productive, and less entitled to a share in direct distribution, than that of the hod-carrier whom he employs. I think that this is scientifically inaccurate, — almost absurd.

The two great facts of the present industrial era are organization and invention. These are the triumphs of mind, and to neither of these do the socialistic philosophers do justice.

The modern method of industry requires that production be carried on upon the large scale. In great establishments, where many workmen are assembled, where labor is subdivided and combined with the most comprehensive wisdom, the mechanical work of the world is now mainly done. The success of this labor depends on its being wisely organized and directed. It will not organize itself. The laborers have not, thus far, proved themselves capable of organizing and directing their labor successfully. We may hope that they will come to that by and by, but they have not reached it yet. Now the value of the things produced by the mass of laborers — their utility and their exchangeability — depends largely on the intelligence by which the labor that produces them is organized and directed. This organizing and directing intelligence is a great factor in production; it is entitled, then, to a liberal reward for the service which it renders to labor. And, as a matter of fact, it is this intelligence that reaps the principal reward. It is not capital, it is management that is carrying off the prizes to-day from the fields of industry. If the manager has capital of his own, he may use it profitably, but it is the management more than the capital that gives him success. Many of the great captains of industry hire their capital and pay low rates of interest for it, then hire their labor and make large profits on that. The capital gets small returns; the lion's share goes to the manager for earnings of management. Now I think that this manager might well be content, in many cases, with smaller gains, but I know not how he can be prevented from receiving a large reward, nor do I see any reason why he should be. The supremacy of mind is a great fact; I do not know how we are going to get rid of it. We had better not try to get rid of it. It is much better to seek in every possible way to put ourselves in possession of the mental equipment which gives power. If the laboring classes want a large share in the product of their own industry, let them seek the intelligence that will qualify them to organize and manage their own industry. That will give it to them, and nothing else ever will.

The other great fact of modern industry is invention, and this is a fact which the socialistic philosophers do not seem at all to comprehend. What they have to say about machinery shows that they totally misconceive the whole case. Machinery, Rodbertus says, is simply intensified labor. "All implements," he reasons, "are *vorgethane*

Arbeit, labor already performed, accumulated labor. When a person uses an implement in a productive operation, he is calling out actively the labor of the present and of the past. The prehistoric man first increased the efficiency of his labor. He then had time left, after satisfying his wants, which he devoted to the making of his first tool. Production in all its stages is only a repetition of this process." That is to say the machine, when it is completed, represents simply the labor of the machinists who made it. That is his theory. It represents much more than this. It represents the thought of the inventor. The machine is organized intelligence, intelligence expressed in terms of physical force. The mind of the inventor is incorporated in its structure. Through this machine the mind of the man who conceived it lays hold on some kind of natural force, gravitation, heat, electricity, and harnesses it and subdues it to the service of man. "I have found out," the inventor says, "a way by which the powers of nature may be made to work for your benefit." Society thinks it wise to encourage such discoveries, and therefore gives this inventor control, for a space, of his own invention. Any one who uses his machine or his process must pay him for it. Part of the product of the machine goes to the laborer who operates it, part to the manager of the business who owns it, part as royalty to the inventor and his heirs. The right of inventive mind to receive a reward for the service which it renders to society is thus recognized by the state. The state is the gainer by this concession. Perhaps when the social state gets itself organized, inventors will be allowed no such rights. This is probable, for I have never found in any socialistic theory any recognition of the justice of such a claim. If that is the policy of the social state, it is doubtful whether there will be many inventors.

This, then, is the first criticism that I have to make upon Socialism as a social theory. It ignores or depreciates the function of mind in production, — the organizing mind and the inventive mind. It puts muscle above mind, and brawn above brain. That is not civilization, that is barbarism.

The second difficulty with Socialism is practical rather than theoretic. The theory that it proposes is too vast for human power. The nationalization of all our industries is its programme. That is to say, it requires the state to take possession of all the lands, the mines, the houses, the stores, the railroads, the furnaces, the factories, the ships, — all the capital of the country of every description. Officers of the state will organize and direct all these industries; will tell the farmers what and how much to plant, and the miners what their output shall be, and the manufacturers of all sorts what and how much they shall produce. A vast army of statisticians will be kept at work discovering what are the needs of the people, and the laboring masses will be employed in producing the goods that will supply these needs, and in transporting them to the places where they are needed, and in storing them, and distributing them to those that need them. What an enormous undertaking it must be to discover all the multiform, the infinite variety of wants of sixty millions of people, and to supply all these wants, by governmental machinery! What a tremendous machine a government must be which undertakes, in a country like ours, to perform such a service as this! The first thing it has to do is to discover some rule for the remuneration of labor. It has undertaken to supply every one with work, and it must know how to pay its workmen. First, it must fix what it calls a normal working day. Rodbertus, curiously, thought it should be ten hours long; most of his modern disciples think that too long. Then it must calculate, in every calling, how much a normal day's work would be. Actuaries and experts must figure up exactly how much a man ought to do in a day, in every conceivable branch of industry; in the carpenter's trade, for instance, how many feet of pine lumber a man should plane in a day; how many yards of three-inch flooring he should lay down; how many mortises and tenons of such and such sizes he should make, and every detail of the carpenter's business must be reduced to a tabular statement, so that a man could tell, on figuring up at night, whether he had done a normal day's work or not. Could any such tabulation be made? They say that a man by the name of Peters actually did it, for the carpenter's trade, at the instance of Rodbertus; but nobody knows whether his tables were accurate or not, nor how they would have worked in actual practice, for nobody ever tried them. But imagine the difficulty of reducing every sort of labor to scale in this way. Possibly it might be done in the carpenter's trade, yet how could it be done? for in every job there are new operations, such as never were performed before. And in multitudinous callings the conditions vary so greatly, the things to be done are changing so constantly, that the attempt at such a calculation would be preposterous.

Yet the whole socialistic scheme depends on making some such tabulation as this for every calling. It looks to me like an impossible undertaking. Nothing short of omniscience could compass it.

Marx proposes, instead of this, to fix, as the standard, common unskilled labor, like that of a man digging dirt; and then all kinds of skilled labor are to be regarded "as multiplied skilled labor, a given quantity of skilled labor being considered equal to a greater quantity of unskilled labor." But this standard who shall fix? And then how shall we reduce the various kinds of skilled labor to the standard? Professor Graham asks these pertinent questions: "Confining ourselves in particular to the different kinds of labor in the factory, all of which are above this unskilled labor, how are we to reduce them? We must first reduce the labor of the ordinary operative to it. But by what rule? How much is it to be rated above average labor? Then comes the skilled labor of the manual sort; this has to be reduced to average labor. Is it to be twice or thrice, and why? Then, where intelligence is of importance, how is the labor into which it enters to be expressed in terms of average labor? — the labor, *e. g.*, of the foreman and overseer, or of the clerks who must correspond in foreign languages, or finally of the owner or manager, whose work in organizing or directing is altogether intellectual or moral? And yet all these laborers are required to produce the final thing, or, what is equally necessary, to find a market. All the labor must be rated in hours of common or average labor, or we cannot tell what it is worth on Marx's principle; and if we do not know its value, we cannot tell the value of a given portion of the product, nor by consequence how much of it the different workers can get in exchange for their certificates for hours of work." [1]

It is the stupendous difficulty of making any such computations and reductions that has driven some of the Socialists, Mr. Bellamy, for example, to adopt the communistic principle of distribution — giving to every person an exactly equal income. But that principle violates the eternal law of justice — "to every man according to his work." I do not believe that any society will very long endure which ignores this law. To say that the veriest idler and shirk, who spends most of his time in evading work and in sponging upon his neighbors,

[1] *Socialism New and Old*, p. 194.

shall have exactly the same reward that is given to the most industrious, the most skillful, the most public-spirited citizen, is to confound every principle of equity and turn the moral order upside down. The universe is not built on that plan.

But having achieved the impossible task of devising a rational and scientific method of distributing the wages of labor, the next thing to do is to find out exactly what everybody in this whole country wants of everything, and how much of it; and then to set the workmen at work to raise it or manufacture it. What an amazing proposition! What a stupendous machine, I repeat, the government must be, to which such a task could be committed! Is it not evident that it would be crushed by its own weight?

Èven if the mental power to frame such a governmental machine were available, we may reasonably fear that the moral integrity requisite for its operation is yet wanting. Such a government would require a civil service a good deal better than ours is or soon will be. "In order to be successful," says Herbert L. Osgood, "the socialistic state would require a standard of public and private morality far above the average attained in our best communities to-day. Official life must be freed from all corruption, from all tendencies to self-seeking, self-indulgence, or greed. Party government would have to undergo important restrictions and limitations. Patriotism must exist among the people to a degree now realized only by a few during a great national struggle for liberty. The average man must be so highly developed morally that he will be ready to sacrifice personal gain and enjoyment for the good of the community. To this age, a system with such requirements can be only a dream, an aspiration."

So, indeed, Rodbertus said. He was wiser in this, as in most things, than many of his successors. The first philosopher of modern Socialism, he was the greatest of them all. He thought that the world must wait at least five hundred years for the advent of the socialistic commonwealth.

But will it not, at length, come true, this dream of the great-hearted philosopher? Doubtless, as Coöperation must await the development of the Coöperative Man, in like manner Socialism must await the development of the Social Man. But have we not a right to look for him? Is not his day coming, by and by?

Doubtless the progress of the human race will be in this direction. Men will learn, more and more, as Mr. Sidgwick says, to consider their industrial work, whatever it is, as a social function only rightly performed when the interests of their associates, and of society at large, are cordially regarded. Men will become more and more willing to sacrifice personal gain and enjoyment for the good of the community. If there is any such thing as human progress, it lies in this direction. May we not, then, expect that the hopes of the Socialists will one day be realized? Possibly, yet

I doubt it. When the Social Man arrives, I doubt if he will be a Socialist. When the Millennium comes, I do not believe that Karl Marx will be recognized as its prophet. And my reason for this disbelief brings me to the last of my criticisms upon Socialism, — that it undervalues character. Its main interest is creature comfort. A better distribution of the *good things* of this life is what it is after, mainly. Of course, it attacks the vices of the present competitive régime, yet chiefly because they hinder the prevalence of plenty.

I quite agree with the Socialists in their indignant repudiation of that doctrine of *laissez faire* which forbids the strong to help the weak, and substitutes the law of natural selection for the law of philanthropy. Doubtless there are duties that All-of-us owe to The-weakest-of-us; and *noblesse oblige* will never cease to bind the hearts of God's nobility. But the problem in all this philanthropy is to help men just enough, and not too much; to help them in such a way as to stimulate their self-respect and strengthen their manhood. We may lift the impotent man to his feet; but it is best to say to him then what St. Peter said, "Silver and gold have I none;" go to work now, and earn them for yourself.

Now Socialism is a natural and justifiable revolt from the unsympathy and hardness of *laissez faire*, and it flies to the opposite extreme, as all reactions do. It undervalues self-help as much as the old régime has overvalued it. The old economy insisted that nothing should be done for anybody; Socialism is inclined to demand that everything shall be done for everybody. The old system left a multitude to be crushed under burdens that they could not carry; Socialism takes away the burdens that are necessary for the development of strength.

Socialism undertakes to furnish every man with work. It undertakes too much. It removes from the individual the responsibilities and cares by which his mind is awakened and his will invigorated.

Not only would it weaken him by taking off the pressure of needs that proves so good a discipline, it would cripple him by limiting in a thousand ways his liberty. M. Godin, in his "Social Solutions," quotes from some socialistic philosopher of the early period his programme of the social order: —

"The constitution and laws regulate all that concerns the citizen; — his actions, his property, food, clothing, lodging, education, work, and even his pleasures.

"The aliments are regulated or prohibited by the law; also the number of repasts, their time, their duration, the number of dishes, their kind and the order of their service.

"All are clothed, nourished, and lodged the same. The republic cultivates and produces all the aliments.

"The law determines the trades and professions to be exercised and all the articles to be manufactured; no other industry is taught or tolerated, as no other fabrication is permitted.

"All the houses are on the same model. The law determines the number and the style of all the furniture of each house."[1]

It is not customary for socialistic philosophers to be so explicit as this; and we may easily admit that this one has carried his passion for equality to an extreme statement; yet the probability that a national system of production and distribution would result in the enforcement of some such uniformities as these, and therefore in the most careful inspection and regulation of all our lives, is not to be gainsaid. To most of us this would prove somewhat burdensome. The interest of your neighbors in your affairs is one of those good things of which there may easily be too much. Who would wish to live in a society in which everybody's conduct was everybody's business? Personality has its own domain, within which intrusion is intolerable, and it is wider than Socialism allows. And I suspect that many an honest workingman, growing restive under the restraint and espionage thus imposed, would be heard crying out, "You have given me bread, but you have taken away my manhood. I can live on a crust and water, but give me liberty or give me death."

In short, it seems to me, as I try to study out the socialistic programme, and to see what its actual workings would be, that it exaggerates the prin-

[1] Page 37.

ciple of solidarity as much as the old régime exaggerates the principle of liberty. It might increase the aggregate amount of wealth, though I doubt it; it might distribute what was produced more evenly; it might secure a higher average of creature comfort; it might multiply commodities; it would not produce men. Scant room and small stimulus would it furnish for the development of high character. Above the dead levels of mediocrity its sons and daughters could not rise. The growth of the highest manhood demands, to my thinking, more liberty and more responsibility than Socialism allows.

And this is the final and fatal objection. Whatever else we get or lose, we must not fail to secure the enduring good of character. The test of all institutions, of all systems, is this: what kind of men do they produce? Socialism would not abide the test.

The competitive régime tends, as we have seen, to produce "a race of powerful incarnate selfishness." Against this tendency every lover of his kind is called to do battle with all the manhood that is in him. Such an issue is simply the consummation of depravity.

> "Not for this
> Was common clay ta'en from the common earth,
> Moulded by God and tempered by the tears
> Of angels to the perfect shape of man."

But Socialism, rushing to the other extreme, seeks to inaugurate a social order that would almost surely produce a race of weak, insipid, dependent creatures. Not such as these are the sons of God, for whose manifestation the whole creation groaneth and travaileth in pain until now.

Midway between these two opposing errors is the safe path of social progress. What is called the golden mean is sometimes a pinchbeck evasion, but here it is not so. And the glory of the latter day will not come until men learn how to unite and coördinate Individualism and Socialism, — how to join liberty with love and the perfection of each with the welfare of all.

X.

CHRISTIAN SOCIALISM.

In most of the recent treatises on Socialism we find a chapter entitled "Christian Socialism." Is the phrase significant? Is Christianity in any sense socialistic, or may Socialism be Christian?

We have found some reasons for believing that Christianity is not Individualism. During the last century the Christian religion has encountered no deadlier foe than the philosophy which underlies the competitive system. The growth of an unsocial temper, so pathetically deplored by Mr. Sidgwick, the separation of classes, the war of interests, are the legitimate offspring of a doctrine which counsels all men to seek first the gratification of self, and trust that all things needful in the way of spiritual and social good will be added unto them. It is evident that the Ricardian economy can be adjusted to no philosophy but that of egoistic hedonism; and it is scarcely necessary to say that this variety of hedonism is the antithesis of the Christian ethics.

The system which exalts competition as the supreme regulative force assumes the law of natural selection. Darwin found his phrase "the struggle for existence" in the writings of Malthus; the survival of the fittest is the logical basis of the old economy. The survival of the fittest means the killing off of the unfit. "There has been of late in some quarters," says Professor Ingram, "a tendency to apply the doctrine of the 'survival of the fittest' to human society in such a way as to intensify the harsher features of Malthus's exposition, by encouraging the idea that whatever cannot sustain itself is fated, and must be allowed to disappear."[1] That is the logic of Individualism.

"But what has Christianity to say about this law?" it may be asked. "Does Christianity deny that this principle of natural selection is at work; that there is a struggle for existence; that it is the strongest, or those best fitted to their environment, that survive? Is not this a fact of science?" The answer is that Christianity does recognize the working of this law, and then sets itself with all its might to counteract the injuries wrought by it; to save those who are being worsted in the struggle for existence. Its King is the first and greatest of those "knights of the long arms," of whom they used to talk in the days of chivalry, whose glory it is to rescue the helpless and the friendless: —

"He comes, with succor speedy,
To those who suffer wrong,
To help the poor and needy,
And bid the weak be strong."

[1] *Encyclopædia Britannica*, xix. p. 373.

Christianity recognizes this law of natural selection as the law of our lower, animal existence, the law by which we are allied to the brutes; and it seeks to hold it in check by the operation of the higher spiritual law of sympathy and good-will. In short, Christianity treats the principle of natural selection exactly as the higher order of evolutionary philosophers themselves treat it. They do not regard it as the final law of a perfected civilization; they show how it operates among the races of animals and plants; they admit that barbarous tribes of men are largely under its sway; but they insist that man is gradually rising above its domain, and that "the end of the working of natural selection upon man" is not far off. "The universal struggle for existence," says Mr. Fiske, "having succeeded in bringing forth that consummate product of creative energy, the Human Soul, has done its work and will presently cease. In the lower regions of organic life it must go on; but as a determining factor in the highest work of evolution it will disappear."[1] This is the evolutionist's account of natural selection as a force in human history, and his prediction respecting its outcome. "The manifestation of selfish and hateful feelings," says this philosopher again, "will be more and more sternly repressed by public opinion, and such feelings will become weakened by disuse, while the sympathetic feelings will increase in strength as the sphere for their exercise

[1] *The Destiny of Man*, p. 96.

is enlarged. And thus, at length, we see what human progress means. It means throwing off the brute inheritance, — gradually throwing it off through ages of struggle that are by and by to make struggle needless. Man is slowly passing from a primitive social state, in which he was little better than a brute, toward an ultimate social state in which his character shall have become so transformed that nothing of the brute can be detected in it." [1] And this, as Mr. Fiske heartily declares, is the precise message of pure Christianity.

But it may be said that the old economy did not justify the egoistic tempers and practices; it only recognized them as facts, and made its maxims and theories correspond to them. This is not quite true. It either assumed, with Smith and Malthus, that unrestrained egoism would result in universal welfare, or it insisted, with later economists, that the law of supply and demand was an "inexorable" natural law whose severities could not be mitigated by the will of man. Both assumptions are false, and both are mischievous, in that they tend to check the development of those sympathetic feelings which are the natural fruit of Christianity, and on which the welfare of mankind so largely depends.

It is only within recent years that the sharp contrast between the tendencies of the individualistic philosophy and the spirit of Christianity has

[1] *The Destiny of Man*, p. 102.

been manifest. The regimen which develops such unsocial tempers is certainly losing favor with students of social science; and Christian thinkers, especially, are turning with a sharp recoil from the doctrines which bring forth such baleful fruit.

Turning away from Individualism, their faces are set in the direction of its opposite, which is Socialism. And they immediately find that the affiliations of Christianity with Socialism are much closer than with the contrasted doctrine. Some foundation might be found for the claim that Christianity is socialistic in its tendencies. In fact, through a considerable portion of its history Christianity has often been explicitly socialistic, or even communistic in its teachings. The early Christian Fathers, by many of their utterances, sanctioned the most radical agrarianism. "The rich man is a thief," cries St. Basil. "The rich are robbers," echoes Chrysostom; "a kind of equality must be effected by making gifts out of their abundance. Better all things were in common." "Nature created community; private property is the offspring of usurpation," said Ambrose. "In strict justice, everything should belong to all. Iniquity alone has created private property," [1] declares Clement. It is true that this is not their uniform teaching, and many other passages defend private property; nevertheless, the stronger impression made upon their hearers by the impassioned appeals of these early preachers was that

[1] Quoted by Laveleye, *Socialism of To-day*, p. xix.

the Christian law simply tolerated private property, and preferred community of goods. The example of the first church at Jerusalem was also supposed to countenance this view, and by many of the words of Christ and his apostles it was believed to be approved. Surely there can be no doubt that the gracious fraternity of spirit, the unity of feeling, the identity of interest which the New Testament always enjoins and praises are nearer to the ideal of the Socialists than to that of the Ricardians. And if I were shut up to the two alternatives of Individualism, with its fierce principle of the survival of the fittest, and Socialism, with its leveling tendencies, I should take my stand with the Socialists.

There is, then, some justification for this phrase, Christian Socialism. I think Laveleye is rather enthusiastic when he cries, "Every Christian who understands and earnestly accepts the teachings of his Master is at heart a Socialist, and every Socialist, whatever may be his hatred against all religion, bears within himself an unconscious Christianity." I would rather say that every intelligent and consistent Christian approves of the end at which the Socialists are aiming; and that, in many of their ideas and methods, Socialists and Christians are in closest sympathy.

We go part way with Marx and Rodbertus; then we part company with them. How far can we wisely go with them? How many of their projects may we safely adopt?

Socialism, as we have seen, is simply a proposition to extend the functions of the state so that it shall include and control nearly all the interests of life. Now, I take it, we are agreed that, as Christians, we have a right to make use of the power of the state, both in protecting life and property, and in promoting, to some extent, the general welfare. Not only have we no scruples against availing ourselves of these political agencies for securing the general well-being, we believe that this is one of our most imperative and most religious duties. Count Tolstoï's philanthropic nihilism does not, probably, commend itself to our common-sense. We think it desirable that all men should be Christians; and we believe that if all men were Christians, the government of this country would be in the hands of Christians, and we cannot imagine that it could be in better hands. The more there is of genuine Christian influence and Christian principle in the administration of government, the better the government will be. That is our claim. Our problem is to christianize all our governments as speedily and as thoroughly as we may. Following this purpose, how far ought we, as Christian citizens, to go in seeking to promote the public welfare through political action? Especially ought we to favor the attempt on the part of the state to improve the condition of its poorest and least fortunate classes? This is the real motive of Socialism. The promotion of the common good is always the end proposed; but those whom it chiefly seeks to benefit are those who are neediest. This is the very spirit and purpose of Christianity; why, then, should not we who are Christians, as fast as we get into our hands the power of the state, use that power for the benefit of the toiling and suffering classes? Why should not "All-of-us," acting through those organized methods which the state furnishes, extend help and encouragement to the weakest and humblest of us? All will admit that there is much that the state can do to improve the condition of its neediest classes, without any straining of its functions.

1. Protection the state does surely owe to all its citizens, rich and poor, capitalist and laborer; concerning this there is no controversy. We may all unite in insisting that the state shall make justice swift and sure. "To establish justice for all men, from the least to the greatest," is the first of its duties. It is doubtful whether there is in all parts of the country an equal law for rich and poor. The friendless poor man gets short shrift and summary vengeance; the rich rascal can secure delays and perversions of equity, and often goes scot free. The man who steals a ham from a freight car goes to jail; the man who steals the railroad goes to the United States Senate. Now, while it may be denied by some that the law ought to do anything to help or favor poor men, it must be allowed by all that the law ought to give the poor man an equal chance with the rich, and this he has not, so long as there is any color of truth in complaints like these.

2. We can also demand that the state shall cease to create and foster monopolies. If it cannot prevent the growth of monopolies, it can certainly refrain from planting and watering them. The state has done a great deal of this vicious husbandry. Its representatives have granted, for no consideration, the most valuable franchises to great companies and corporations, and the money of these great companies and corporations has shaped legislation and purchased judicial decisions by which their power has been confirmed, and by which the tribute they levy upon the industry of the country has been legalized and perpetuated. We have been furnishing these people rope wherewith to strangle us. We have suffered our national domain, by hundreds of millions of acres, to fall into the hands of monopolists. All this legislation, establishing and fostering monoplies, is especially burdensome to the poorer classes. We must all pay tribute to these lords of our own creation, but it is harder for the poor than for the rich. The street railways in most of our cities ought to bring large revenues to the municipality, by which the burdens of taxation should be greatly lightened. Instead of this, every workingman with his dinner pail pays toll to a rich corporation. The monopoly of the public land is a special hardship. This has always been the poor man's refuge. The main reason why labor has steadily commanded higher prices in this country than elsewhere has been the abundance of cheap and

accessible land to which the wage-worker could at any time betake himself if wages were low. Now that this door is shut, the pressure upon the working class is sure to increase. It is time for the Christian citizen to take hold with resolute hands of these abuses of government by which the poor are despoiled and burdened and fettered for the benefit of the rich.

So much as this we can all agree upon. That the state shall furnish to its humblest citizen perfect protection; that it shall establish equal and even-handed justice; that it shall refrain from licensing and fortifying monopolies; that it shall do what it can to give all its citizens an equal chance; all this the devotee of *laissez faire* asserts as strenuously as the scientific Socialist. But this, says the philosopher of *laissez faire*, is the place to stop. Protection is the legitimate function of the state; the promotion of welfare is not. It is not wise to enlarge the field of state action. Much of the work that the state now does is poorly done; it would be folly to put any more work into its hands. The Socialists' demand for extension of the functions of government is the extreme of folly.

This argument is familiar; I have used it myself, more than once; but it is not so conclusive to my mind now as once it was. It is by no means clear that our governments would not all be improved by putting heavier burdens on them. Satan finds *some* mischief still for the idle hands of public officials.

In my own city the power of the mayor is almost all taken away and distributed amongst various boards; the office, as an executive, is as near a nullity as the Legislature could make it; and the consequence is that no man of high character wants to take it, and it is a source of scandal and public shame. The Legislatures of many of our States have tried this experiment of stripping the people of the cities of political power; the attempt has been made to take as many as possible of the functions of government away from the people and confer them upon outside commissions; and the result has been, in every case, disastrous. The weaker the municipal government is, the wickeder it is: is not this a universal rule? If much responsibility is concentrated upon one person, the people are much more likely to see to it that that person is fit to bear it. The heavier the duties resting upon the officials, the greater the care exercised by the voters. And I am not at all sure that a considerable extension of the functions of government would not arouse our people, as nothing else has done, to attend to their political duties. At any rate I am quite ready to see the experiment tried. If we have not yet attained to that lofty morality by which we should be fitted for the tremendous tasks imposed upon us by Socialism, we are ready, I think, to assume larger responsibilities, and to undertake greater services. It may be that some inspiration would come to the people, if by any means their notion of the scope and dignity of their political functions should be somewhat enlarged. The theory of *laissez faire* is that the state is to exercise only police functions. Now the duties of a policeman are not of a particularly inspiring nature. It is doubtful whether they tend to enlarge his intellect or improve his manhood. I seem to remember the fragment of a classic ode, in which is some suggestion that a policeman's life is extremely unideal. If, now, the people, in the exercise of their political duties, are in the habit of regarding themselves simply as policemen, it is doubtful whether they will get much mental or moral stimulus out of politics. The infusion of other motives might lift our political life to a distinctly higher plane. It is easy to sneer at sentiment in politics; you know of some high-class journalists who are masters of this art; and, on *laissez faire* principles, this sneering is, of course, the proper thing; but there is still room for doubt whether desiccated politics are altogether nutritious to the national life. And if the American people should leave these rudiments of political science, and go on toward a higher conception of their political life, regarding, with Bluntschli, "the proper and direct end of the state as the development of the national capacities, the perfecting of the national life, and finally its completion,"[1] I should begin to look for the dawn of the informing light upon our political chaos.

In the most curt and comprehensive fashion, let

[1] *The Theory of the State*, p. 300.

me proceed to name a number of the points at which, according to my conception of the Christian ethics, the functions of the state might well be extended beyond the boundaries laid down by the advocates of *laissez faire*. Concerning some of these governmental interferences, there will be no question; they are already sanctioned by the traditions and the laws of our people. Yet they are all departures from the strict standards of Individualism.

1. The Christian state may furnish a certain amount of public instruction, and require its citizens to avail themselves of it. This is not, of course, an open question in this country, albeit the measure is utterly socialistic. So Mr. Herbert Spencer and his friends most strenuously declare. The provision of elementary instruction for the common people at the expense of the state is denounced by them as a most dangerous encroachment upon liberty. In the eyes of these gentlemen the common school is one of the most startling signs of the loss of our birthright. When a free people submits to be taxed for the purpose of providing educational opportunities for all its children, it is taking a long stride, so Mr. Spencer and his friends cry out, in the downward way from freedom to bondage.

I do not sympathize with their apprehensions, but I quite agree with them that the measure is essentially socialistic. It is true, that awkward attempts have been made to justify our public schools on the ground that they prevent crime; but, with President Walker, "I do not believe that this was the real consideration and motive which, in any instance, ever actually led to the establishment of the system of instruction under public authority, or which, in any land, supports instruction now. . . . In all its stages this movement has been purely socialistic in character, springing out of a conviction that the state would be stronger, and the individual members of the state would be richer and happier and better if power and discretion were taken away from the family and lodged with the government."[1] The only thing to be desired is that this work of public instruction should be distinctly and consciously placed upon this higher basis. It is not well done when it is done as a mere extension of the police function of the government. It needs a higher motive.

2. The sanitary supervision by which pure air and water are secured for all the people is another of the functions of the Christian state. Professor Walker thinks that this is fairly included within the police functions; that it is simply a measure of necessary protection; Mr. Spencer would scarcely agree with him; nevertheless, whether it be old or new theory, it is good sense and good Christian morality.

3. The Christian state can discourage, if it cannot extirpate, the parasites which are fattening

[1] *Scribner's Magazine*, i. 110.

upon our industries. (1.) The criminals are parasites of labor; all theories of the state agree that they must be repressed. But there are other parasites toward whom a wholesome severity is required. (2.) The pauper class is rapidly growing, and it is fostered, in large measure, by careless administration of poor relief. The question whether the state ought to undertake the support of the helpless poor is an open question; but there is no question concerning the attitude of the state toward that large class of persons who would rather beg than dig. For all this class it must learn to provide sharp restraint and rigorous discipline. To live without work at the expense of the community must be made hazardous and unprofitable business. (3.) The gamblers, including the crowds of so-called speculators in the great cities who get their living by betting on margins, are also parasites; economically they belong to the same class as the beggars and the thieves; they live without rendering to society any service whatever. These classes absorb a large share of the wealth produced. Whatever they consume is so much subtracted from the aggregate product of industry, and it leaves just so much less to be distributed among the productive classes. The state must find some way of suppressing this economical parasitism.

4. The Christian state will find itself enlisted for the suppression of the saloon. Under the theory which limits the power of the state to the suppression of crime and the preservation of the

liberty of the citizen, this might be logically admissible; under the theory which commits the state to the promotion of the general welfare it is easily justified. Whatever manifestly tends to the detriment of society at large may and must be suppressed. The liquor interest has become a gigantic, consolidated, unsocial force, directly and malignantly assailing the community, undermining its thrift, corrupting its political life, destroying its peace; and against it, not merely the teacher with his science, and the preacher with his Bible, and the philanthropist with his sympathy for the fallen, but "All-of-us," with all the power we possess, must arise and do battle. Of course, it is important that we manage this campaign with that prudence which is always the better part of valor, and that we carefully consider all the conditions in choosing our weapons and our methods of attack; but there need be no uncertainty as to the ultimate purpose, which is the destruction of the rum power, — the power that now is threatening the destruction of the state.

In these instances which I have last named, — the destruction of the parasites of industry and the overthrow of the liquor power, — it is the *general* welfare that is sought, rather than the welfare of any particular class; yet the evils against which they seek to provide bear most heavily upon the poorest people; and it may, therefore, be claimed that through such measures the strength of the state is interposed to shelter or succor its weakest citizens. This is a socialistic motive. This is Christian Socialism.

5. A more express interference of this nature is the prohibition of Sunday labor. In this action the state puts forth its power for the benefit of a particular class, the laboring class. The suppression of Sunday labor is a plank in the platforms of many of the socialistic and labor organizations of Europe. It is a purely socialistic measure. And I, for one, am Socialist enough to be heartily in favor of it. The one priceless good of which the workingman ought never to be robbed is the weekly rest day. It cannot be preserved for him without the interposition of the state. As Dr. Leonard Woolsey Bacon has so strongly shown, the liberty of rest for each requires the law of rest for all. It is probable that some revision of the Sunday laws of most of our States is necessary to fit them to the new conditions of civilization; but the line should be sharply drawn, and every industry that can be interrupted by the Sabbath should be brought to a pause every Saturday night.

6. I have no doubt that the state will also be compelled to limit the hours of labor in some callings, if not in all. With respect to the wisdom of such restriction upon the labor of women and children there can be no question. The fact that the machinery now in use in the various manufacturing industries will produce vastly more than the people can possibly consume, if it is kept in operation through all the hours of the present working

day, indicates the wisdom of reducing the number of those hours. The simplest method for the accomplishment of this purpose may be the direct interference of the state. When "All-of-us" see that it is best for "All-of-us," "All-of-us" can say so and have it so. It is very often said that all these matters will regulate themselves if they are let alone. But they do not regulate themselves; the tendency to the degradation of the weak is irresistible. "The free play of individual interests," says Dr. Henry Carter Adams, "tends to force the moral sentiment pervading any trade down to the level of that which characterizes the worst man who can maintain himself in it. So far as morals are concerned, it is the character of the worst men and not of the best men that gives color to business society. . . . Suppose that of ten manufacturers nine have a keen appreciation of the evils that flow from protracted labor on the part of women and children, and, were it in their power, would gladly produce cottons without destroying family life, and without setting in motion those forces which must ultimately result in race deterioration. But the tenth man has no such apprehensions. The claims of family life, the rights of childhood, and the maintenance of social well-being are but words to him. He measures success wholly by the rate of profit, and controls his business solely with a view to grand sales. If, now, the state stand as an unconcerned spectator, whose only duty is to put down a riot when the strike occurs (a duty which government in this country is giving up to private management), the nine men will be forced to conform to the methods adopted by the one. Their goods come into competition with his goods, and we who purchase do not inquire under what conditions they are manufactured. In this manner it is that men of the lowest character have it in their power to give the moral tone to the entire business community." [1]

This is not mere theory; this process has been repeated over and over for a hundred years; and we have seen the weak oppressed and degraded by it, and workmen and work-women by the thousand sinking into starvation under the operation of this law. This is what liberty means when the weak are left to contend with the strong. And no remedy for this state of things arises under purely economic causes. On the contrary, it waxes worse and worse continually. The only remedies are the combination of laborers to resist such oppression and the intervention of the state. Both remedies are necessary. The state has interfered, with excellent results, to protect women and children, to prescribe the length of the working day, and, in many ways, to check the rapacity of the worst employers. Such legislation does not abolish competition, but it fixes certain limits within which competition shall take place. It does not cancel liberty; but when it finds men using their liberty for the destruction or the enslavement of their fel-

[1] *Publications of the Am. Economic Association*, i. 505.

low-men, it lays its restraining hand upon them. The state comes in, with its intelligence and its conscience, to protect its weaker members from the greed that would pauperize or degrade them. The liberty of the few rapacious employers, who are forcing all the rest to adopt their inhuman methods, is somewhat restricted; the liberty of the employers of good-will, and of the whole class of employees, is greatly enlarged and confirmed. I cannot regard this as a tyrannical proceeding; and it seems to me that those who so characterize it are juggling with words and shutting their eyes to facts.

7. The Christian state must also, for the same reason, enforce the sanitary inspection of factories, workshops, and mines, to make sure that the health and the safety of laborers are secured. And it would be well if the definition of "factory" could be so extended as to include those small garret shops in the cities in which so many lives are destroyed. This is a service which the intelligence of the nation owes to its toiling classes. Legislation of this sort has been in force for several years in Great Britain and in this country. It is pure Socialism, Christian Socialism, but it is none the less wise and beneficent.

8. The Christian state has a great service to perform in healing strife, in making and publishing peace. It ought to stand forth as the peacemaker in the quarrel between the employers and employed. When the employer is an individual

or a private company, perhaps the best thing that the state can do is to tender its good offices to assist the parties in coming to an understanding. To this end it may wisely furnish models and suggestions in certain rules of permissive legislation for the arbitration of labor disputes. It may appoint in every county, or perhaps in every large judicial district, a tribunal before which such disputes may be brought. To point out by such permissive legislation the right method of submitting such disputes to arbitration, and thus to open the path of peace and invite the contending parties to walk in it, may be a useful service. Such legislation as this has been provided, with good results, in some of our States.

In the case of all quasi-public corporations, such as railroad and telegraph companies, there ought, I think, to be a stringent rule requiring all labor disputes to be settled by arbitration. Such corporations stand upon a different footing from private companies or individual employers; they have derived from the state their franchise; they have received from the state certain large powers and prerogatives; they may properly be controlled by the state in that part of their administration which directly affects the public interest. There ought, therefore, to be in every State a judicial tribunal armed with full powers for the settlement of difficulties between these corporations and their employees. To this end, the associations of employees should be incorporated by the state, and the corporation thus formed could be treated as a responsible person, and punished for any failure to obey the decision of the arbitrator, by mulcting its treasury or canceling its charter. The failure or refusal of either party to submit to arbitration should be made a punishable offense ; and no railway company should be entitled to military protection until it had shown its willingness to settle its difficulties with its men by the methods of peace. Pending this settlement, the men should be required to continue their work on the former terms, and it should be made a misdemeanor for them to interrupt or obstruct in any way the work of the company. The duty of the Christian state should be to put an end to these miserable feuds, and to compel those at least of its citizens who are engaged in these public services to compose their quarrels without resorting to force.

I am also enough of a Socialist to believe that every Christian state ought to seek to enter into the most solemn treaty stipulations with every other nation, providing that all international disputes shall be settled in the same way by reference to neutral and friendly powers. I do not believe that it is either necessary or wise for this country to be spending millions on millions of money in building war-ships. There is a more excellent way. The United States is in a position to preach and enforce this gospel of peace among the nations ; a resolute and persistent effort to avert and banish the possibilities of war by establishing and maintaining the tribunals and the methods of arbitration is the best service that this Republic can render to the commonwealth of nations.

9. Certain great enterprises for the promotion of the public welfare the state may wisely undertake. Before those who insist that state administration is always clumsy and costly stands the Post Office as a constant confutation. A more efficient or more benign and humane agency for the service of public needs it would be difficult to conceive. It is almost as cheap as light and air and gospel grace. If this business had been committed to private enterprise, we should very likely be paying five or ten cents, instead of two, for the conveyance of our letters.

It is difficult to understand why the telegraph service, which is far simpler and more manageable, should not also be controlled by the government. With even our present civil service, which is far from perfect, I doubt not the expense of telegraphic communication could speedily be reduced one half. The people are paying to the owners of the principal telegraph monopoly a good rate of interest on four or five times the actual cost of the lines it is operating. I see no decent reason why "All-of-us" should allow Some-of-us to bleed The-rest-of-us after this fashion. That the state should provide the people with facilities of communication by telegraph, as well as by post, I have no doubt.

Whether the railroads will speedily come under state control or state ownership is a more difficult question. If, as has been said, the question simply is whether the government shall own the railroads or the railroads the government, the choice will not be difficult. As to the principle involved, the state has the same right to build and maintain a railroad that it has to build and maintain a highway. If the public welfare would be greatly promoted by committing this great interest to the control of the state, then it ought to be done. The objection to it is the fear that the state would fail in the administration, and be debauched by it. The common theory is that private enterprise manages all these great matters much more economically and efficiently than the government could manage them. This is not clear; the reckless and wasteful competitions of the railway builders are notorious. We are told that the present railway facilities of the United States could be replaced for a thousand million dollars less than they have cost. And the extortion, the tyranny, the corruptions practiced by these great corporations in their discriminations against persons and places, in their cold-blooded slaughter of the enterprises which they cannot control, and in their manipulation of courts and legislatures, furnish one of the most harrowing chapters of recent history. Just what can be done about it is not so clear. It is a great and difficult problem. But it is not solving itself; *laissez faire* shows no signs of solving it. The evils connected with railways in this country manifest all the symptoms of a social disease, whose constant tendency it is to become more aggravated and unmanageable. It is a desperate case; it may require surgery; but that is not a good reason for letting it alone. A Christian state that sought the highest welfare of its people would be constrained to take hold of it. The one strong reason for hesitation is the fear that the state is not Christian enough; that the public virtue is not sufficiently genuine and stalwart to cope with such a problem. If the people think themselves too weak to challenge the evils that threaten their national life, doubtless they are too weak. But who will save them? They must find for themselves some way of deliverance. To my own mind, it has become increasingly clear that all industries which are virtual monopolies must be controlled by the state. Railroads, telegraphs, street railways, gas companies, electric lighting companies are all, in effect, monopolies. In the business which they do there can be no effective competition. The railroads compete at certain points, but the traffic at non-competitive points is therefore taxed to pay for the low rates at the competitive points. By the discrimination which they are able to make in behalf of persons and places, the railways may be and often are gigantic instruments of oppression; their policy is to favor the strong at the expense of the weak. And it is evident that any industry in which there is and can be no effective competition should be under the control of the state.

Such an industry has abandoned the field and the method of commerce. It is not under the law of supply and demand; it does not offer its commodities or its services in an open market; it has closed the market; it compels you to take what it offers and pay its price. This is not, in any proper sense, trade; this is essentially taxation. Now I do not think that a free people can safely commit the power of taxation to irresponsible associations of their own citizens. And, therefore, I think that all virtual monopolies must eventually belong to the state. It is not necessary to confiscate them, they can be equitably acquired without inflicting real injury on their present owners. Nor is it necessary that the state should undertake the management of these great industries; it may simply fix the rates and the rules of service, and then lease them for limited terms to the highest bidder, — regulating and superintending their work, as that of the national banks is now regulated and superintended, but leaving to private enterprise their administration. All this, as it seems to me, the Christian state is bound to do, as part of its duty to the weak in protecting them against the encroachments of the strong.

10. One or two measures of public policy may, erelong, commend themselves to the judgment of "All-of-us." Professor Hadley has shown, in a recent paper,[1] that the evils connected with our railway system are closely paralleled by those aris-

[1] *Quarterly Journal of Economics*, vol. i. No. 1.

ing from our great industrial corporations of all kinds; and that the treatment found necessary in the one case may possibly be called for in the other. And President Walker, in the article quoted above, sets forth in a few luminous words the portentous nature of the problem presented by the corporation, that artificial person created by the state, "whose powers do not decay with years; whose hand never shakes with palsy, never grows senseless and still in death; whose estate is never to be distributed; whose plans can be pursued through successive generations of mortal men." The creation of this gigantic immoral person wholly neutralizes the operation of the ordinary economic forces; with a "magnified, non-natural man" of this description no ordinary person can compete on any terms of equality. Here enters a power that requires for its control the supreme power of the state. None other dares confront it. How to enchain and subdue this race of titans that we have let loose in the land is a great question which the Christian state is called to solve.

The nationalization of the land does not, probably, commend itself to the good sense of the American people, but they are pretty sure to find out, in the discussion now in progress, that the supreme title to the land is vested, by the Creator, in the people; and while they clearly see that private ownership most surely promotes the public welfare, they are also likely to insist upon a sharp limitation of the amount which any individual is allowed to control.

And, finally, inasmuch as the creation and continuance of enormous fortunes is clearly against public policy, the Christian state may find it wise to lay a heavy tax upon all legacies exceeding a certain sum. The rights of every man over his possessions — no matter how acquired — terminate with his life; the privilege of bequest is granted by society because it is believed that thrift is thus encouraged, and the public welfare promoted; when it becomes evident that the perpetuation of great properties is injurious to the people, ways must be found of discouraging such accumulations.

Such are some of the changes in their methods of administration which a Christian people, intent on promoting the general welfare, may seek to realize. It is needful, first, to see what ought to be done in this direction, and how to do it. Statesmanship is an art — the finest of the arts; Christian statesmanship ought to be the highest type of this finest art. The Christian people of this country are called to rule; a great curse will rest on them and on the land if they come short of their high calling. If they are to rule, they must know how to rule. Not only the office-holders, but the people also must know how to rule. There is a right way to rule a state as there is a right way to sail a ship or to plant a field, and the Christian people must learn that way, and practice it.

It is sometimes supposed, or seems to be, that if the people are only spiritually minded, the affairs of the state will order themselves aright by a spontaneous movement. It is a vast mistake. Here is a farmer planting his corn in the middle of August, because he has been taught and believes that that is the proper time for planting. Of course he never gets a crop. Shall we say that if the man were soundly converted his methods of husbandry would be wiser? It is not his heart that is wrong, but his head. It is not the gospel that he needs; he needs a few primary lessons in agriculture. Here is a physician who has been taught and believes that the right remedy for consumption is blood-letting. His patients all die, but he keeps right on with his bleeding, ascribing their death to a mysterious Providence. It is not the lack of religion that ails him; he has too much religion and too little science. Even so the great art of statecraft, like the lesser arts of husbandry and healing, must be studied by the men who practice them,— studied patiently and profoundly,— else they will continually be making ruinous blunders, and no sanctification of the heart will prevent or correct these fatalities. They must not only mean well; they must know how. It is not enough that their hearts are right; their heads must be clear and their methods wise. And when Christian men set themselves to the study of these great problems, they need to understand at the outset that their Great Teacher and Guide is not Machiavelli the Italian, or Bentham the Englishman, but Jesus Christ the Nazarene. The fact that he has in this world

"A kingdom still increasing,
A kingdom without end,"

is the one fact that they must not miss. To know well the laws of that kingdom, as fully as we can to make the laws of our States conform to them, — this is our problem. To apply the Christian law to all our social and political questions, and to walk steadfastly in the light of that great law in all that we do for the state and for society, — this is our rule of life.

This is what we have been trying to do in the studies that are now closing. We have diligently sought to discover the bearing of this law upon these great social problems; and we have found its precepts writ large over every one of them. I hope that we may be able to see that Christ has a law for the government of men in the social relations, and that it is our business to enforce that law; not merely to tell men that they ought to be Christians, but to show them the principle on which they must act when they become Christians.

Yet the fact remains that Christianity is something more than a law; it is a spirit also, and a life. The trouble of the world arises in part from the fact that men have not fully comprehended Christ's law in its application to social relations, but even more from the fact that they have failed to receive his spirit and to share his life. We need better methods; still more do we need better men. Bad philosophy has slain its thousands, but bad temper its tens of thousands. There is need of reform in economical theories, and industrial systems, and in political machinery, but deeper is the need of devoted and sanctified souls. It will be of little avail to reorganize our industries if we cannot secure a more unselfish spirit in employers and employees; arbitration will fail unless the love of justice can prevail over the greed of gain; industrial partnership will come to naught where the egoism of the old régime remains unsubdued; coöperation will never thrive until the coöperative spirit and habit have found root in the lives of men. So, also, all these efforts of the state, of which we have been speaking, to redress social injuries, and promote the social welfare, will be futile unless a deeper sense of the sacredness of their political obligations and a stronger love for social justice can, somehow, be imparted to the citizens. Thus we see how all the evils of which we speak have their roots in moral causes, and how all the radical remedies must come from an improvement in the moral standards and the moral conditions of men.

Yet here is a troublesome antinomy that we must not fail to see. From "the reign of peace, the happy republic," cries Professor Graham, "what chiefly keeps us back? Want of love and charity," he answers; "too much regard for self, too little regard for others, the latter partly a consequence of our present condition of life and scheme of society. But society will change, is changing, and if social arrangements, which at present repress and smother the native love in our hearts for our fellows, were corrected, this innate love would get its chance and would shine forth."[1] If men were better, the social arrangements would soon improve; but while some social arrangements remain as they are, it is hard for men to become better. The best teaching, the holiest example, the most inspiring influence would avail but little for the reformation of a family packed into one of those horrible tenement houses of New York; you must get them out of those associations. Men need mending, and their circumstances too. The Individualist cares only for men and neglects the environment; he is a fool; for the environment, in a thousand ways, reacts upon the man and checks or distorts his development. The Socialist cares only for the environment, and neglects the man; he is a fool; for the springs of power are in the human personality. You cannot make men temperate by law; and if your teaching gives the impression that the evil of intemperance is wholly or mainly due to the presence of temptation, it will be very mischievous teaching. It is the men that most need reforming. Nevertheless, it is far easier to reform men when the temptations are lessened — remove them utterly we never can; and therefore we must labor steadily at both ends of the line — to save men and to banish temptation. A better society to live in, and better men to live in it, — this is what we are working for. And so we come

[1] *The Social Problem*, p. 468.

back to the point from which we started, and listen once more to the voice of our great Leader and Captain, as he cries, "Repent, for the kingdom of heaven is at hand!" To help in the utterance of that message, in the fulfilling of that promise, is the high calling of every Christian man. It is the faith, also, of every Christian man that this is no quixotic undertaking, but that the increasing purpose which he discerns is leading to the goal of universal peace. He believes that this great realm of natural powers can be christianized; that its worst abuses can be corrected; that its mighty forces can be sanctified; that industry and trade can be so transformed by humane motives that they shall be serviceable to all the higher interests of men. There are evidences that this work is going on silently but effectually; that some of our captains of industry are beginning to understand something of their true vocation, and to see that it is not alone their individual advantage that they ought to seek, but the welfare and happiness of all whose labor they employ. Faint signs are even now visible in our sky of the dawning of a day when business shall be to many men the high calling of God and the medium through which unselfish spirits shall pour out their energies in ministries of help and friendship; when political office shall be regarded as a solemn trust held for the welfare of the whole people; when the creatures who live by corrupting and despoiling their fellows shall seem to men's thought almost as fabulous as the dragons and vampires of mythologic lore. I write these last words while the Christmas bells are ringing and the happy voices of little children, with their hearts full of the gladness of good-will, are borne to my ear upon the frosty air. Surely it is a happier world than that to which the heavens bowed that night in Bethlehem! And is there not good reason for hoping that

> "Love which is sunlight of peace,
> Age by age [shall] increase,
> Till anger and hate are dead,
> And sorrow and death shall cease"?

It is not all a dream; the happy time draws nearer with every circling year. Speed it, all powers of earth and air and sea; run with its messages all men of good-will; let its morning star shine upon your banners all children of the light; to its glad music, now faintly heard, now clearer growing, march to the battle all soldiers of the cross; till its light shall shine on every land, and in its peace and plenteousness all the sons of men shall rest and be satisfied.